OCEAN

Mackenzie
Bay

135 130 125 120

NUNAVUT

65

Mackenzie R.

Norman Wells

Great
Bear Lake

Mountain R.

NORTHWEST
TERRITORIES

Great
Slave
Lake

Willow Handle
Lake

MACKENZIE
MOUNTAINS

Yellowknife

YUKON
TERRITORY

ANA
ACIER Whitehorse

60

Juneau

BRITISH
COLUMBIA

ALBERTA

115

120

135 130 125

moving**waters**

ADVENTURES ON NORTHERN RIVERS

SAM COOK

Sam Cook

Stone Ridge Press

Stone Ridge Press
2515 Garthus Road
Wrenshall, MN 55797
218.384.9856
www.StoneRidgePress.com
sparkystensaas@hotmail.com

MOVING WATERS
ADVENTURES ON NORTHERN RIVERS

Printed in Altona, Manitoba Canada by Friesens
10 9 8 7 6 5 4 3 2 1   First Edition

Jacket Design: Laurie Kania
Map Illustrations: Matt Kania [www.MapHero.com]
Editor: Craig Lincoln
Photos: Sam Cook

ISBN-10   0-9760313-5-3   hardcover
ISBN-13   978-0-9760313-5-2   hardcover

For
All of my paddling partners, who understand the
call of wilderness rivers

ACKNOWLEDGMENTS

First, as always, I thank my wife, Phyllis. She was my paddling partner on that first northern river trip, the Gods River, in 1983. We've paddled a lot of miles together since. I couldn't ask for a better partner, in the bow or in life.

I thank all those with whom I've shared canoes and camps on these far-flung trips. They are not only excellent paddlers and good in the woods, they are one fun bunch. I see them in the flames of campfires wherever I go.

I appreciate my employer, the Duluth News Tribune, which enabled me to make all of these trips in the first place. Portions of some stories in this book first appeared as part of newspaper accounts of the trips. A big thanks to Craig Lincoln for his sensitive editing that only a fellow paddler could pull off.

Finally, I thank John Stone and Don Wenger, who first showed me the North.

Sam Cook
Duluth, Minnesota
January 11, 2007

A huge thanks to "the Map Hero," Matt Kania who produced the beautiful map of the North for the end pages. His talented wife Laurie produced the stunning cover. Sam's good friend Craig Lincoln masterfully edited the text and arranged the essays so they flow.

The Publisher wishes to thank Sam for his enthusiasm for the project as well as for meeting every deadline. I've had the joy of reading Sam's articles and books for 25 years. We are very fortunate to work with a writer of his caliber.

Sparky Stensaas, Publisher
Wrenshall, Minnesota
January 13, 2007

CONTENTS

INTRODUCTION

A fortuitous event occurred in the summer between my soph-
omore and junior years of high school. John Stone, the den-
tist in our small Kansas town, and Don Wenger, a local business-
man, led a trip to the canoe country of northern Minnesota and
northwestern Ontario. I was lucky enough to be one of the
rammy teenagers who went along.

Until that summer, my idea of north had always been
Nebraska. Suddenly, new phrases crept into my vocabulary. The
Quetico-Superior. Border country. The Canadian Shield.

We outfitted through the Charles L. Sommers Canoe Base
near Ely. I had no idea where I was for those ten days in
Ontario's Quetico Provincial Park. All I know is that I ate food
with the occasional mosquito in it, drank water straight from
the lakes and caught fish almost at will. We didn't do any of
those things in Kansas.

I didn't know it then, but those ten days in the wilderness
marked a turning point in my adolescence. They opened my eyes
to the vast and largely roadless country between Minnesota and
Hudson Bay. And they introduced me to a craft that I've been in
love with ever since—the canoe.

That was the summer of 1964. Now, with friends I've come
to know like brothers, I've paddled hundreds of miles on some
of the continent's most beautiful moving water. We have paddled it in the spirit of adventure, with an insatiable curiosity

about what lies around the bend and with a sense of humility toward the land. We aren't out to conquer anything or put notches on our belts. We don't thrive on danger. We aren't addicted to life on the edge. We go because we love moving water, distant horizons and the simple rhythms of life on the trail.

That isn't to say we haven't had some moments that required all of our talent and ingenuity.

The stories that follow represent a sampling of our days on the water. Most of these experiences were accumulated at the rate of one trip per year, the balance of our time given to families and careers and other travels. While most of the accounts represent river trips, some of these adventures took place on flat water. Even on those trips, the water was often moving, in both a literal and figurative sense.

Most of us are in our late 40s to late 50s now, and we're still at it. This doesn't surprise us. We expect, perhaps naively, to be at it much longer. A man I know calls our annual pilgrimages to the North our "regression trips."

"You do those trips because you think you're younger than you really are," he said.

Maybe so. But I think we have a pretty realistic picture of who we are and what we're capable of. I imagine we'll be doing this as long as we can swing the paddles and heft the packs.

But I won't deny we're chasing something in our past at the same time. I know I am. I'm just a kid from Kansas who discovered the Quetico-Superior in '64 and is still amazed at how much North there is.

LEARNING ON THE FLY

S ure we were green. Ken Gilbertson knew that, and he let us
go anyway.

Gilbertson was director of the fledgling Outdoor Program at
the University of Minnesota Duluth. He was certified as a whitewater canoe instructor. He had taught wilderness first aid. He
was the only one who really knew what he was doing.

It was Gilbertson who had come to Phyllis and me months
before and told us the university was offering a month-long trip
to the Gods River in northern Manitoba. The year was 1983.

"You ought to come," he said.

So, Phyllis and I had gathered around a table at UMD one
evening with Ken and Rob and Jerry and Ross and Jim and Peg
and laid the plans.

A month? How did we ever swing that? Granted, none of us
had kids yet. Still, a month is a long time for working folks. But
this was too good to pass up. A dream trip. Paddling to Hudson
Bay. Whitewater. Brook trout. Possibly polar bears. We would
be following in the footsteps of famed newscaster Eric Sevareid,
who immortalized the route in his classic book, *Canoeing with
the Cree.*

Gilbertson figured he could teach us to paddle whitewater as
we went. And the Gods, he knew from his research, was a for-
giving river. The water wasn't cold. The rapids were manageable.

"We'll stop at the first set of rapids and practice for half a day," he said.

So we paid our 600 dollars—food, gear, canoes and gas—and signed on the line.

The fact is, if you wait until you are fully prepared and equipped before you tackle any big undertaking in life, a lot of adventures would never happen. At some point, you have to make the leap, launch yourself into something that may be a bit over your head and see what happens. As an Ely dogsledder told me about taking such risks, "One of two things can happen. Either it works out, or it doesn't."

Gilbertson and I were talking about that trip not long ago.

"I can't believe how little we knew when we did that," he said.

Sometimes it's best not to know what you don't know.

Truth is, we pulled it off with hardly a hitch. Okay, there was the matter of the wheel bearings burning out on the trailer somewhere near Winnipeg. Yes, we inexplicably completed the trip with a surplus of 23 boxes of crackers. And Peg did come down with a nasty case of Giardia toward the end.

But we ran all the whitewater right-side up. We caught big brookies. We made the infamous Bayly Portage. And in the drizzle and gray of an August evening, we set our eyes upon Hudson Bay.

I have tried to remember, when my kids have come to me with less-than-sound plans for questionable adventures, that they, too, will probably return in one piece.

Once on the water, we learned to paddle at a small chute of whitewater where the Gods River flows out of Gods Lake. Gilbertson taught us our draw strokes and pry strokes, how to catch an eddy and peel out of it, how to make an upstream and a downstream ferry. We swamped two canoes as we practiced, but that didn't count. The canoes were empty. We were just practicing.

It must have looked fun. A bush pilot who had just flown in to the lodge there came out to shoot the drop with Ken and his paddling partner, Bob Engelson. They delivered him safely downstream.

We spent three weeks on the water, including a week just getting to the river, and paddled 250 miles. The mosquitoes and black flies were fierce. The rapids were all we wanted. The fishing was at times sensational.

We learned that the Cree villages along the way were living dichotomies, with life divided between the best of traditional life with the worst of contemporary life. We saw a moosehide being smoke-tanned over a smudge. From old women, we bought hand-sewn moccasins and mitts adorned with intricate beadwork. But we also had an eight-year-old ask us, "Do you get high?" And we learned that alcoholism and paint sniffing were chronic problems.

What we came to know best was the river and the sky and the delicious pace of life on the trail. We knew what Sevareid was talking about in *Canoeing With The Cree* and what Sigurd F. Olson had described in his book, *The Lonely Land*, an account of an expedition on the Churchill River.

We came to know what all the travelers before us knew, that there is no life better than that of a voyageur, whose panorama changes with every bend in the river. We knew the ache of shoulders and arms after long pulls down big stretches of water. We knew what it meant to be ravenous three times a day. We knew how fast sleep came when every fiber of your body was weary.

We also knew the joy of making a camp where possibly nobody had ever camped before. We came to know the satisfaction of picking through a boulder garden of rapids rock by rock. And we discovered the pleasure of being on the trail long enough that the calendar became irrelevant.

In short, it was the trip of a lifetime.

What we didn't know then is that it would spawn a lifetime of trips.

BREAKING LOOSE

PRE-TRIP BLUES

Something strange happens to me two or three nights before any major wilderness venture. Most of the trip's details have fallen into place by then. The food is bought and packed. The canoes are rigged and ready. The piles of gear in the basement have been refined and pared down to the essentials. All that's left is to throw things in the packs and load up.

That's when a melancholy feeling comes over me that I can't shake until we're finally on the way. It happens every time.

Until that time, the trip has been a set of dates in my mind, a week or two blocked out on the calendar. Now it's real. I'm going to walk out the door early some morning soon and not see my wife and the kids for too long. I feel sad. I still want to do the trip. I know it will be good. But the thought of being away from the people I love more than anyone else on the planet weighs heavily on me.

And I suppose, to be honest, there's some guilt at work here, too. I probably don't fully appreciate what I'm asking of Phyllis, holding things together at home, working outside the home, squiring the kids to soccer games and dental appointments. It's a big job when there are two of us around. And now, here I go, off to have fun in the woods.

The guilt is in there somewhere. But the dominant emotion I feel is sadness.

I used to assume I was the only one this dark cloud hung over on the eve of a trip. Then I mentioned it to my traveling companions. Those with kids said the same thing. They've all felt the leaving-home blues. We all accept that this is a part of forging off to remote places, doing things that come with some inherent risks.

For a couple of nights before a trip, I'll look in on my son and daughter after they're asleep. I just look at them, maybe touch my son's soft little arm or rub my daughter's hair. I just want to see them, remember them, focus on how much they mean to me. And sometime in that last day or two before the trip, Phyllis and I will steal away for a couple hours. We'll hike a trail or sit by a river or go out to dinner, just to connect one final time before the trip.

None of this takes away the melancholy feeling. But these rituals seem to help.

Several years ago, when I got a new whitewater paddle with a white blade, I asked my son and daughter to each draw something on it. I wanted to take along something that would remind me of them when I was far away. They were happy to accommodate me. With a purple permanent felt-tip marker, my daughter, an avid cross-country runner, drew a running figure and wrote, "Running is Cool!" beside it. My son, always eager for a fresh canvas, drew me a moose, a basketball goal and a seal balancing a ball on its nose.

Then, several hundred miles from home as the canoe approaches the lip of a rapids, I glance down at those drawings and remember my most important mission of the trip: Get home. Seconds later, my partner and I are swept over the drop. Reactions take over. The well-decorated paddle assumes its primary purpose.

Occasionally, in the evening on a trip, I'll get to missing my family. It will happen when I'm by myself, looking at the water. Suddenly, the river blurs and I'm yanked back home. I wonder if I'm missing a soccer game that night, or a barbecue with friends, but I give up wondering. Out on the river, I have lost contact with the calendar. I have no idea what Phyllis and the kids are up to. I send some good thoughts their way, maybe sing them a quiet song, and head back for the campfire.

Such moments of longing are rare, though. Most of the time, I'm so immersed in the experience that there's little time left to think about home. Even in the long daylight hours of the Canadian north in July or August, the evenings evaporate. Dinner, dishes, maybe a quick clean-up, some photos in the low light, a little time to write in the journal, and then exhaustion from the day's paddling sets in. Time to slither into the bag, kill any mosquitoes that followed me into the tent and call it a night. If I know before the trip that the moon will be out, I always remind Phyllis and the kids to look up at it and know that I'll be looking up at it, too.

Of course, I wouldn't have to go off to paddle wild rivers, leaving my family behind. It's not like it's a requirement. None of us would have to. But if we didn't, something inside of us would wither and die, I'm afraid. I am not sure what part of my soul is fed when I am on a river, but it is a part that gets nourished in no other way.

The sadness I feel upon leaving for a wilderness trip is more than offset by the joy of returning home, tanned and bug-bitten, to reclaim my family. When the kids were younger, they would come racing out of the house and down the sidewalk to throw themselves around me. Arms around my neck in a death-grip hug, legs wrapped around my waist. First one child, then the other. They looked fresh and new, as if I could have forgotten what they looked like in ten days or two weeks.

Phyllis is usually more restrained. She manages to keep her feet on the ground when we embrace. But it is as if I'm seeing her in a new light as well.

I never try to unpack the day I arrive home. It's too crazy. I stack the stuff on the porch and go inside.

We all have stories to tell.

ON THE ROAD

Only the paper carriers are stirring at this hour on a July morning in Duluth. It's 4:00 A.M., maybe 4:30. Light is just beginning to seep into the sky over Lake Superior.

In ones and twos, the eight of us have found ourselves in Dave Spencer's driveway. We're here to load boats and cram Duluth packs into two rigs. Sometime later that afternoon, 600 miles north of Duluth, we will fly into Manitoba's Bloodvein River.

Around us lies all we will need for eight days on the river—bulging Duluth packs, a stack of paddles, stuff sacks of lining ropes, daypacks with personal gear. We greet each other warmly despite the hour.

How many times have we done this over the years? Almost once a summer for fifteen or twenty years, give or take a river. It may be familiar, but it never gets old.

Every trip has its sweet moments, and this early-morning gathering is always one of them. Finally, all of the list-making and preparations are complete. Canoes have been rigged and repaired. Gear has moved from piles on the floor into pudgy Duluth packs. Paddles, life jackets, spray skirts, food packs—everything is here and ready.

Though we may be sleepy, we are all full of anticipation. We have no idea what lies before us. Will the water be high or low? Will we forget something important and have to improvise? Will the bush-plane flights be smooth or rough? Will the fishing be good or poor? All of that will unfold in time.

For now, we are happy simply to be here once more. About the time the birds begin to sing, we're loaded and on the road.

I suppose it would theoretically be possible to embark on one of these journeys at 10 A.M. or noon or sometime in late afternoon. But we favor the early start. Pass the Thermos of coffee. Switch drivers in Warroad or Winnipeg. Shuffle places in Dick Adams's Suburban so no one has the middle seat too long.

Oh, we've had a few shaky starts. On this trip, Tim Bates was bed-ridden with the flu until a day or two before the trip. He seems okay now, but we'll make sure he gets plenty of rest on the way up.

One year, Mike DeBevec of Grand Marais barely made it to our early-morning rendezvous because of several stream washouts along Minnesota's North Shore highway. Must have been quite a storm, we figured. It wasn't until two weeks later, watching television in an Edmonton motel on our return, that we learned the storm had leveled thousands of acres in Minnesota's border country.

Someone forgot a cooler full of meat as we embarked on another trip, and we didn't realize it until we were 75 miles down the road. Too late. We would just have to catch more fish once we were on the river.

We nearly always drive north—eight, fourteen, sixteen hours. On a few occasions, we've flown. Either way, we ultimately end up at some tiny bush-plane base on the edge of the wilderness. Thompson, Manitoba. Lynn Lake, Manitoba. Pickle Lake, Ontario. Norman Wells, Northwest Territories. Chitina, Alaska.

A friend of mine, who packs his kayak and heads for simple places in the Caribbean and Central America, says, "I know I'm getting to a good place when there are chickens walking around in the airport."

We haven't seen chickens at our jumping-off places, but all of the bush-plane offices are similar. They're often tiny places, usually in some prefabricated building. A huge map covers one wall, a composite of smaller maps that have been pasted together. In the middle of the map, there's a pushpin. It's the "you are here" point. From the pushpin, a string hangs soiled and limp. It's there, ready to be stretched to any potential destination, to help pilots compute distances.

Sometimes, we find a clerk behind a desk, but other times, we've found nobody at all for a couple of hours. No sweat. We're on trip time now. We pull out books. Or we peel down and go for a swim off the dock. Maybe we pull out some food and munch.

We know how to wait.

Next thing we know, a Beaver or Twin Otter is taxiing up to the dock. Looks like our ride is here.

SOME ASSEMBLY REQUIRED

Alaska's Tana River flows cold and gray from under the Tana Glacier in the Wrangell-St. Elias National Park and Preserve. It's a powerful river from the very beginning, with a fast current, a heavy load of glacial silt and big rapids. At our camp just a few miles below the source of the river, it was already a half-mile wide.

Fourteen of us were making an exploratory raft trip down all thirty miles of the Tana and on down another seventy on the Chitina. It was June of 1995. The trip had been organized by the Outdoor Program at the University of Minnesota Duluth.

Our second day in camp at the headwaters, half of our crew hiked upstream to see the glacier, while the rest of us remained in camp. Those of us left behind would begin assembling the frames and inflating the three rafts that would carry us downriver.

The day dawned clear and warm. Randy Carlson, Dick Adams, Dave Spencer and I sat along a snowmelt feeder stream and began sorting out raft parts. We had all the big wooden frames and the bolts that secured them. We had all the nylon webbing we needed to lash the frames to the rafts. But, wait ... Where was that third set of oarlocks?

We double-checked all the bags of raft gear. Nothing. Carlson, our trip leader and director of the Kayak and Canoe Institute at UMD, walked back up to camp to see if we'd left another bag up there. Nothing.

Slowly, reality sunk in. We had three rafts but just two complete oarlock rigs. Things grew pretty quiet as the four of us sat there contemplating our dilemma. Somehow, we had to find a way to row that third raft.

We somehow had to invent heavy-duty spacers to secure the oarlocks above the raft frame. We had pins, the heavy steel shafts that are bolted to the frame and to which the oars attach with metal clips. Without some way to hold the oarlocks above the raft frame, they'd be useless to us.

We could all see what the challenge was. Carlson, an excellent leader and a master of the positive frame of mind, stood up.

"Well," he announced. "We're going to be okay. We need to go up and look around camp for some materials."

And off we went. We found some polyvinyl chloride (PVC) pipe and cut some spacers. That would help. But we needed something thick and solid, something with a hole down its center through which each pin could pass, something that would hold up to the torque as we tightened the bolt on the pin.

Somebody suggested that a thick slice of a spruce trunk might do the trick, if we could only find some way to drill a 5/8-inch hole through its center.

"Ready to go to Menards?" Carlson asked.

We knew it was technically against park rules to cut a tree down, but we figured this was an extenuating set of circumstances. We used a camp saw to remove two cross-sections of a spruce tree about six inches in diameter. Then used Leatherman tools, a screwdriver and a Buck hunting knife to bore holes dead center through our discs of spruce.

It took all of us four hours to improvise our oarlocks. They looked pretty good, we had to admit. But the real test would come when we launched the rafts and leaned into the oars. That moment came two days later, when we slid all three rafts into the river. Carlson was at the oars as the current caught our raft. He braced his legs against a cross-member of the raft frame and heaved on the oars. The pins groaned against the spruce—and held. Carlson cranked on the oars to move the raft across the river. The raft responded.

The main emotion in our raft was relief. We still had over a hundred miles to go before we were out of the woods, but we were no longer worried.

And if our repairs failed, there were always more spruce trees at Menards.

THE LONGEST CARRY

With every step, the soggy earth tried to swallow my boot. I'd been carrying the canoe so long I felt as if a pair of German shepherds had jaw-holds on my shoulders. We had started this portage at 9:30 A.M. Now it was almost two in the afternoon.

Eight of us on the way to Hudson Bay were making the Bayly Portage, two miles of quivering bog under the heat of the July sun. The portage, from tiny Bayly Lake to sprawling Gods Lake in northern Manitoba, has a reputation in wilderness canoeing circles. Eric Morse, a noted Canadian paddler who made many trips with Ely's Sigurd Olson, dubbed the carry "one of the worst portages I can recall" in his book *Freshwater Saga.*

"It was through a muskeg swamp and without shade," Morse wrote. "Every step was into water."

We started the portage after breakfast on Bayly Lake and a short paddle up a beaver flowage. The first few steps were on dry land, and we wondered if the stories we had heard about the portage were true. Soon we were plodding through the muskeg, which tried to suck your boots off with every step. The day was clear and warm, and in the open bog the heat was oppressive. For some reason, perhaps low humidity, the black flies that had plagued us on previous days were not a factor.

Each of us was responsible for two packs, or a pack and a canoe, but it was impossible to carry both loads at once. We would sink too far into the bog. It's difficult to describe how much effort each step required. I recall vividly watching my L.L. Bean boot meet the bog mat, then disappear as the boot plunged into the ooze and the bog engulfed my foot. That was the easy part of each stride. The hard part was trying to pull your boot free of the bog's sucking grasp.

Several times I went in up to my knees, but I was lucky. Phyllis, my wife, twice found holes in the bog and plunged waist-deep. She would have to slither out of her Duluth pack, extricate herself from the bog and sling the pack on again.

Jim, another member of our group, thought there was enough water beneath us that it would be easier to tow his Kevlar Mad River canoe over the bog than carry it. He was wrong. After plodding a few hundred feet dragging the canoe, he gave up and threw it back on his shoulders.

Most of us were in good physical condition. We already had been on the trail for several days and were in that groove where you feel fit and strong. But Bayly Portage, with the relentless sun above and the porous bog below, wore us down.

The trail was long and straight, no doubt a highway for snowmobilers traveling between villages in the winter. I remember carrying the canoe as far as I could before the lactic acid turned my legs to mush. I'd drop the canoe and look back to see the food pack waiting for me where I'd shed it.

Each of us was lost in his or her own world on the carry. We would pass each other coming and going, but there was nothing to say. We were so dispersed over the portage that if one of us went into the bog, we were on our own to find a way out and move on. I remember being thirsty but having little to drink. We must not have filled our water bottles—or enough of them—before starting the portage. We didn't stop for lunch.

Because we each had to shuttle two loads across the carry, the two miles became six. When we reached a swampy backwater of Gods Lake at 2:15 P.M., the water looked brackish and nasty. As thirsty as we were, most of us wouldn't drink until we had paddled out onto the main body of the lake.

Morse recalled exactly what he did when he had completed the carry:

> *Eventually, we hit the end of the portage where the smokers flopped down and lit up. My own reaction at this point, I am told, was to hand my watch to someone and then walk, fully clothed, into the cool lake.*

Our group made camp that night on the north shore of Gods Lake, which is sixty miles long and about twenty miles wide. We were famished, of course. It was Ross and Jerry's turn to cook. They never truly embraced their cooking chores, but this night was by far their most memorable failure. They cooked up a huge pot of what was supposed to be macaroni and cheese, but the cheese had an odd, clumpy look to it. It seemed to cling to the macaroni noodles in viscous globs rather than melting and attaining a sauce-like consistency.

"Where'd you get that cheese?" Peg asked.

Jerry held up a bag he thought was powdered cheese.

"Those are the powdered eggs," Peg said.

We have always referred to that meal as egg-aroni. And we ate every bit of it.

A GOOD RIVER IS HARD TO FIND

The DeHavilland Twin Otter banked south, leveled out and made its final descent to Willow Handle Lake. The lake is near the headwaters of the Mountain River, which dashes down through the Mackenzie Mountains of Canada's Northwest Territories to its confluence with the Mackenzie River.

Few of us in the cargo hold of the Twin Otter had made a bush flight like this before, skipping over barren, 7,000-foot peaks and craggy canyons. We were more accustomed to the Hudson Bay lowlands, where the contour lines on our topographic maps rarely ran close to one another. These were real mountains, and we would soon be paddling a river that plunged an average of twenty feet per mile as it tumbled down the flanks of this range. Along the way, the Mountain would bull and swirl its way through six canyons whose sheer walls rose 600 feet or more from the river's edge.

Willow Handle Lake lay emerald green in a seam among these mountains. The Twin Otter taxied on its floats approaching a makeshift dock used occasionally by hunting camps nearby. The pilot cut the engines at just the right moment—how do they make that look so easy?—and the plane swung broadside, nudging the rickety dock.

One by one, the six of us from Minnesota and Wisconsin climbed out to behold the world around us. Mountains reared their heads on all sides of us. The haze of forest fires softened the ranges. Here, close to the treeline, the peaks were barren rock and rubble up high. Their lower reaches wore aprons of vegetation—willows and smaller shrubs.

This was alpine country, lean and spare. Wildlife, we would learn, is hard to come by here. A few bands of Dall sheep. The occasional lone wolf. A few unseen grizzlies. We wouldn't see a raven for several days.

We knew this was grizzly country, but we didn't think our chances of seeing one were particularly good. That perspective had changed when we talked to our outfitter at Norman Wells before our flight. We asked him how often paddlers on the Mountain see bears.

"About half our groups see one," he said, hardly looking up from his paperwork. "A lot of groups have had to pack up and move their camps farther downriver."

We had pondered that pronouncement silently until I asked how far downriver a group might have to move in that situation. The outfitter looked up.

"You'll know," he said.

Now, at Willow Handle, we unloaded our packs and canoes, and the Twin Otter took off, the whine of its Pratt and Whitneys reverberating off the peaks. We watched until the plane banked east and disappeared in the haze. Few silences are so profound as the kind that follows a floatplane's departure deep in the wilderness.

We would be eleven days and 175 miles on the river, and we wouldn't see another human. Quiet country up here.

We spent the extended daylight of the northern summer installing kneeling pads in our rented canoes and casting flies for Arctic grayling in the lake. The grayling were cooperative. Dan Theis and Dave Baumgarten each caught several of them before supper.

The next morning, we rose early to go find our river. We had seen it from the air on our way in, a trickle of current reflecting the sky among the knee-high vegetation. The lake drained into this trickle, we had been told. But as it often is with things we had been told before other river ventures, reality on the land-scape didn't quite match up. Which is to say, Willow Handle Lake didn't drain directly into a burbling brook that would eventually become the rollicking Mountain River.

At the downstream end of the lake, our three canoes fanned out, seeking an outlet. Nothing obvious presented itself. Eventually, we beached our canoes and went exploring in groups of two. The lake didn't drain so much as it seeped into a low bog. We wandered aimlessly about the bog for probably half an hour, looking for the river. We found a damp spot here and there, but nothing resembling current.

But this had to be the place. Everything went downhill from here. The country was big, and we lost track of each other occasionally. Or, you'd look up and see a couple of your partners far across the valley, two splotches of color amid the vast green.

Finally, we found a miniature river, not quite a canoe-width wide. It wasn't impressive. A meandering rivulet, narrow enough to jump across. We trudged back to Willow Handle Lake to retrieve our gear and made the portage to this hint of a river. Then we began lining and shoving the canoes down the waterway.

But within a few minutes, our little river dried up. Rather, it braided itself into smaller and smaller channels until each was absorbed by the boggy lowland.

We got out and went looking for something more substantial. Again, we all split off in different directions. We had been searching for several minutes when we heard a voice. It was Dick Adams, off in the distance.

"Here it is," he shouted.

His voice sounded tiny, swallowed up by the vast country. We portaged our canoes and gear over to where he was and found something approaching a small stream. It had a lively current. It was barreling down the valley at a good clip.

We loaded the canoes again and began wading them downstream, our feet and ankles growing numb in the icy current. Within half a mile, the tributary seemed to gain volume. The course widened. We hopped in and began paddling. The stream described continuous arcs as it meandered through the valley. At one point, we passed a shelf of ice perhaps a block long, dripping its frigid meltwater into our flowage.

After an hour or so of paddling, we joined another tributary. This one was gray-green with silty mountain run-off. It was a couple of canoe lengths wide. It was the real thing. We pulled over at a gravel bar and lashed on our spray skirts.

We had found the Mountain River. Now we were looking for the Mackenzie.

Mood Swings

Highs and Lows on the Bloodvein

We clambered out of the canoes to see if the skimpy rock outcropping offered the potential for camping. To be honest, it looked pretty ugly.

But at this point, we couldn't afford to be picky. We had been on the Bloodvein River for ten hours and covered seventeen miles. We had run eight or nine sets of rapids and lined two or three others. We had also made three portages, the last one at 5:30 P.M.

We knew, having paddled the river eleven years earlier, that a nice campsite awaited us tonight. It was on a high bluff, and the river danced along below in an unrunnable set of rapids. We were tuckered when we got there.

But we could see bodies moving about. A scout group was camped there. Rather than portaging through their camp, we worked back upstream a half mile to this rock outcropping.

It was one of those places that looked, from a distance, as if it could be a camp. Upon closer inspection, we could see it was a dismal little spot. Too little rock outcrop. No decent spots back in the woods to pitch tents. No flat spot for the fire grate.

We looked at each other as we explored the woods. It was clear nobody had ever camped here before. No fire-blackened rocks. No obvious tent pads.

Oh, well. It would just be for a night. We started carrying gear up from the canoes. Dan Theis and I considered several poor options for our tent. Eventually, we cleared a couple of popple deadfalls and pitched the old Marmot tent on an undulating piece of ground covered with knee-high bushes and sapling jack pines.

The others pitched their tents out on the edge of the rock spit on inclines that would guarantee a night of sleeping-bag sledding.

The site was popular, however, with black flies. The evening was hot and humid, and the little kamikazes stirred to life as soon as we set foot in the woods. Hot damn, they must have thought. First blood meal all summer.

I wrote in my journal that night that wolves were howling somewhere in the distance, just audible, but now, two years later, I have no recollection of the wolves.

That's because it rained all night. It was still heavily overcast and raining when we arose the next morning. Ken Gilbertson and Tim Bates and the others had oatmeal bubbling by the time Theis and I emerged from our tent. The eight of us were a depressing sight, standing around in our rain gear, raindrops falling from cap brims into cups of coffee and oatmeal. The black flies, undaunted by the precipitation, hovered around us like dark clouds, zeroing in for an attack when we let our guards down.

Oh, it was lovely.

You learn, over the years, to roll with days like this. It doesn't pay to get worked up about them. Yeah, it would be nice to be dry. Yes, it would be refreshing not to have a black fly up your nose. And yes, it's one ugly little camp. But it isn't forever.

You cinch the cuffs of your rain gear. You gag down the oatmeal as quickly as you can. You purposely don't point out the black fly smashed on Ken's cheekbone. Hey, it looks good there.

What you've come to know is that conditions are beyond your

control. Rain. Tent sites that resemble mine fields. High water. Low water. Burned-over country. Mosquitoes. Black flies. No-see-ums.

No use wishing things were different. It is what it is. We broke camp and moved downstream, each of us trailing our personal swarm of black flies. We portaged through the scouts' camp and chatted briefly. Dan took a nasty spill on a steep and muddy incline below their camp. He landed sitting up, wearing 85 pounds of Royalex canoe on his head. No harm done.

The gray persisted as we paddled and portaged. The air was thick and still. We stopped for lunch on a rock dappled with goose droppings.

My journal that evening captured the afternoon succinctly:

Next portage around two falls we never saw, just heard. Slippery. Muck. About one-quarter mile. Bad footing. Treacherous lichen on rocks. And extremely buggy with mosquitoes. Multiple bites simultaneously. Involuntary acupuncture.

At the end of the portage, waiting to put in, we were a bedraggled lot.

"The things we do for fun," Dave Spencer said.

Then, at about 3:00 P.M., we rounded a bend in the river and saw a rapids ahead. When we got out to scout it, we saw the point of rocks was an elongated campsite with all that a good camp implied—level places for tents, a perfect spot for the fire, a long spit of rock to catch the wind.

It was a little early to make camp by our standards, but we didn't hesitate. As we unloaded our sodden packs from the sloshy canoes, the sun broke through. A breeze kicked up. Clouds scattered. Sun glinted off the fast water.

In five minutes, the place looked like a yard sale. Rain gear and tent flies and sleeping pads flapped from clotheslines. We spread humid sleeping bags over bushes and tents. We ran the empty canoes through the rapids and pulled them up below. Then Dave and Seth Spencer peeled down to birthday suits and life jackets. We could see the plan clearly. They were going to bob the rapids, a gentle Class II with a few good waves and no problem rocks.

That's all it took. Soon, almost everyone was shooting the rapids, body style, eddying out below and going back for more. It was totally exhilarating—all current and bubbles and buoyancy.

The sun bore down on us, turning our gear crisp again. The humidity must have dropped thirty points in thirty minutes. Miklos Jalics, visiting from Hungary, joined me for some fishing below the rapids. Our scented plastic worms were a hit. Walleyes liked them. Northern pike liked them. A five-pound channel catfish liked them.

We went to a far shore to clean the fish and cube the fillets. Theis prepared fish stew and fry bread for supper. Like mergansers on a rock, we lined up on that spit of granite and looked out over the rapids as we ate.

The black flies were a memory. The warm breeze caressed our bare arms. The rapids chattered below.

Nobody said much for a while. We were hungry.

The mosquitoes asserted themselves at sunset, when the breeze died. We hustled around camp, grabbing bags and pads and clothes from the lines. We dived into the tents and fell asleep listening to the river.

LIFE IS GOOD

The outlook was bleak. We needed a camp, and clearly this wasn't the spot. It was low and wet for as far as we could see, although it had looked decent from a distance. We gathered back at the three canoes. They looked small along the edge of Manitoba's Seal River.

We were three days from Hudson Bay, and the day had turned about as ugly as it could get. We had just finished running a long set of sloppy rapids in the rain. Our canoes were covered by spray skirts, so most of the splash that came over the bow had trickled back into the river. Still, we had been paddling in the rain much of the day, and we were getting soggy.

Near the end of the rapids, we were suddenly struck by a powerful northwest wind. It was so strong, lashing us broadside, that I remember thinking, "Has a canoe ever been blown over by the wind?"

We made the bend at the bottom of the rapids and turned directly into the headwind. Dave Spencer and I dug as hard as we could, making slow progress to rendezvous with the other two canoes. The afternoon was wearing on, and we weren't going to go anywhere against that wind.

Now, our hopes of making a quick camp had been dashed when this campsite didn't pan out. With our hoods cinched tight against the rain and wind, we looked at our options.

"That beach across the river looks like it might be a little protected," someone said.

We decided to make the 300-yard river crossing. We waded out and loaded up as the canoes bucked in the surf. The crossing was a wind ferry. All we did was try to maintain forward progress with the bows of the canoes angled just toward the far shore. Paddling in place, the wind shoved us swiftly across the turbulent surface of the river.

But when our canoes nudged the crescent-shaped beach, the wind was still raging. The lee we had hoped to find was nonexistent. The six of us spread out, working upwind to see if a point of low trees offered any protection. It didn't, and the beach gave way to a brackish lagoon anyway.

"I had resigned myself to eating a cold supper and crawling in the tents to hold them down," Dan Theis would say later.

The idea of even trying to pitch a tent on that beach was daunting. The idea of having to sit inside of it to keep it there was beyond depressing. But we'd been in jams before. Somehow, we could ride this out.

About the time most of us had reached the same conclusion Theis had, Tom Bell came walking through the willows and back to the beach.

"I found a spot that might work," Bell said, "but it's quite a ways back there."

We had little to lose. We pulled the canoes up on the beach and followed Bell. We walked through waist-high grasses and a tangle of willows before beginning to climb into some small spruces. We walked through the spruce for another hundred yards or more, flagging our trail with life jackets hung in trees.

Bell led us to a small opening in the woods near the top of a rise. The opening—lichen-covered bedrock—would be just big enough for our three tents and a fire. The stunted spruces offered just enough protection from the wind to get us by. We were sold.

It was a long carry to get all our gear up there, and going for water was a little unhandy, but none of us complained. In minutes, it seemed, we had two tarps strung to offer protection from the wind and rain. Spencer fired up the Coleman two-burner stove and had a pot of cheese-and-broccoli soup going in no time.

Firewood appeared, along with some curls of damp birchbark. It wasn't long before Dave Baumgarten had a fire built and was toasting his fleece pants over its flames. We pitched the tents almost on top of each other, guylines intersecting guylines. But we were warm. We had soup in our bellies. We had shelter for the night.

Our spirits, as low as they could get on that wind-whipped beach, were now soaring. Supper was macaroni and cheese with dried veggies and sun-dried tomatoes. No meal in the woods ever tasted better.

In some perverse way, I loved the way that day unfolded. Certainly, we don't go looking for adversity, but if you spend enough time on the trail, you'll find it. When it happens, you often have to rely on all your ingenuity and skills to find a solution to the problem at hand. It's a rare pleasure to operate out on the fringes of your capabilities. When you do, and you come through as we did that evening on the Seal, you enjoy a rarefied sense of satisfaction.

Spencer was feeling the same way I was when we crawled

into our tent that night and shook our dry sleeping bags from their stuffsacks.

"That's what I love about canoeing," he said. "One minute, you can be totally miserable, and the next you've got a nice camp, a fire going, soup on the stove, and life is good."

Outside, the wind was still rattling the tent fly.

Off the Beaten Path

The map showed a long sliver of an island just ahead of us.
It looked as if the most expedient choice was to stay river-
right. I didn't bother to mention this to my paddling partner,
David Spencer, in the stern. I had traveled with him enough to
know we tended to look at these decisions in much the same
way. Sure enough, he set our bearing just a touch to the right as
we approached the island.

We were five or six days into a ten-day trip down Manitoba's
Seal River. Six of us were traveling in three canoes. I looked
back to see if the other canoes had chosen to come our way.
One of them had, but Duluth's Tom Bell and Dave Baumgarten,
in the third canoe, disappeared beyond the tip of the island.
They had chosen the channel less traveled.

"I see Bell and Baumgarten went the other way," I said.

This didn't surprise either of us too much. Tom and Dave
aren't always likely to take the most obvious route. If another
choice holds the promise of intrigue, they'll often spring for it.
And I think sometimes they simply like to split off so that as a
group, we'll have covered all the possibilities.

"You wait," I told Spencer. "They'll come across something
unusual and have a story to tell when we see them again."

The island must have been a half-mile long. The water was
flat on both sides of it, so there were going to be no tales of
unexpected rapids to run.

Spencer and I paddled along silently with Dick Adams and Dan Theis in another canoe behind us. It was one of those gray, sullen days when even a wild river on its way to Hudson Bay seems a little drab. Fire had swept through the region in recent years, and the shores were studded with blackened spruce trunks and an understory of fireweed. Hardly postcard material.

Finally, we passed the far end of the island and stopped paddling to let Tom and Dave catch up.

"How was the scenic route?" someone asked them.

"You won't believe it," Baumgarten said from the bow. "A wolf came out from shore and swam across the river in front of us. He wasn't more than fifty yards off our bow."

Just luck. Blind luck. But it's surprising how often good things happen when you get off the beaten path.

One morning on Manitoba's Pigeon River, I awoke early and slipped out of the tent with my camera. Mist was hanging over the set of rapids where we had camped. I wanted to shoot some photos at the lip of the drop in the early-morning sun. I'd been sitting there, watching the light change and shooting a few photos, when a black bear ambled down the far shoreline and began swimming across the river toward me. I kept shooting.

The bruin seemed a little confused at midriver. He must have picked up my scent. He did a complete 360 in the river, then decided he'd better scoot back to the shore he had come from. He couldn't see me, and, still bewildered, set out to cross the river again. But this time, too, he changed his mind at midriver and swam back to shore. He disappeared into the woods.

A nice little moment, away from camp and my paddling partners.

Another time, on the Mountain River in Canada's Northwest Territories, we made camp for the day at 9:40 A.M. because we happened onto a spot so spectacular that continuing was out of the question. It was at the head of the Fifth Canyon, one of six canyons the Mountain River knifes through in the rugged Mackenzie Mountains.

Not long after making camp, Dick Adams and Mike DeBevec went exploring. They headed for a cleft in a rock promontory that rose like an anvil from the river. They took no food. They filed no flight plan. They just meandered off and, once at the base of the ridge, started climbing. The climb looked tough. Adams and DeBevec must have been gone for four hours. When they came shuffling back to our camp on the beach, someone asked them how the climb had gone. Adams, a man who doesn't waste words, provided the answer.

"If anyone wants to do that climb," he said, "I'd suggest you drop down and start doing push-ups until the urge goes away."

But a few weeks later, he showed us the photos he had shot from that peak. It's a safe bet only a few human beings on the planet have pictures like that.

In each of these cases, we were already a few hundred or a thousand miles from home, paddling rivers that see few travelers. You could argue that we were already off the beaten path. So, what it is it that lures some of us even farther? Why do we have to see what's on the other side of the island? Why do we have to rise before dawn and steal away from camp? Why do we see a spire of rock and say, "I need to be up there?"

The answer is simple. We're never going to be here again.

BROOKIES FOR BREAKFAST

T his was not going to be a pleasant camp. We could see that.
Day's end had caught us at a portage around an unnamed
set of falls on Manitoba's Gods River. We'd run several rapids
that day, and we were tuckered. We'd been told by other travelers of the river that we could catch brook trout below these falls.

"You can camp at the top of the portage," one fellow traveler had told us.

We had visions of a beefy rock outcropping, someplace spa-
cious enough to accommodate the eight of us, with good access
to the river. But standing there, looking around in that late-day
stupor that haunts expedition paddlers, we saw no place to pitch
our tents and no obvious place to set up the camp kitchen. What
few rocks there were seemed jumbled and confining. A major
lobe of granite slanted sharply to the water. It was swallowed
there by an eddy below the falls that had more current moving
upstream than a lot of rivers have moving downstream. Scary.

At its upstream end, the eddy met a black tongue of water
that surged over this ten-foot drop with unrelenting fury. The
entire river, usually 200 to 300 yards wide, had been hour-
glassed into this wild chute. The water didn't fall. It shot off the
invisible lip of the falls and thrust itself in one smooth arc into
the pool below. There the river self-destructed in a maelstrom of
clear water and white froth. It gathered itself in that pool and
somehow became a river again farther downstream. The tumult

made conversation at the water's edge difficult.

Away from the river, we were faced with the reality of our camp. A rusted Spam can on a tree branch marked the portage. The carry was littered with pieces of plywood, the hulls of shotgun shells, more cans and refuse. We wandered off in pairs to find places for our tents.

We had become accustomed to humble camps on this three-week trip to Hudson Bay. Rivers that flow to Hudson Bay are rarely known for their classic camps, but we'd pitched our tents in some ugly spots in the two weeks we'd been on the trail. Phyllis and I found a tiny opening between the spruces to pitch our two-person tent. I'm sure nobody had ever pitched a tent there before.

Peg and Jim began whipping up a macaroni and cheese dinner from a fire pit we engineered in the jumble of rocks. The fire smelled good. We picked up and consolidated the trash. The transition from a homely piece of country to home for the night was taking place.

While Peg and Jim prepared supper, I put a pack rod together, snapped a cheap orange spoon on my line and tossed it where the river and the eddy met. The water is exceptionally clear on the Gods, and I could watch my spoon twisting and flopping in the turbulence. Then I saw something else in the water. Brook trout as long as my forearm. Three, four of them. They materialized out of the depths in that crazy water, and one of them inhaled my spoon.

I had fished for brook trout in a lot of places, but I had never seen anything like that. It remains, twenty years later, my most poignant fishing memory. The fish, about a three-pounder,

fought with the spirit and power of a true river fish. It torpe-
doed to the surface and danced across the water. I could see the
fish, but the sounds of its thrashing were swallowed by the roar
of the river. Eventually, I brought the fish to the shore, landing
it awkwardly because the rock slanted steeply to the river's edge.

I held the brookie up and studied it. In the low evening sun at
that latitude, the fish was beautiful. Few other fish can match a
brook trout for sheer beauty anyway, but catching this one here,
in this amazing setting, on our way to Hudson Bay, was almost
more than I could bear. I was ecstatic. Ken and Phyllis came
down to admire the fish. When we had had enough, I removed
the barbless hook of the spoon from its jaw and set the fish
aside. We would keep it for breakfast.

Phyllis had already grabbed my rod and had tossed a gold
and orange spoon into the pool. I don't know how many casts
she made, but I knew something good had happened when I
saw her jumping up and down. Another brookie.

"Four or five of them came after it," she would say later.

The one that took it was a three-pound male, full of fight. It
used the current to its advantage and put a serious bend in the
rod. Phyllis was still shrieking. She finally gained the upper hand
and led the powerful fish to a small notch in the rocks. I lifted it
out of the water and handed it to her. The big male had a belly
the color of the sunset and fins to match. We took several
photos, but I'll confess that the excitement must have gotten to
me. I underexposed all of them.

It was Ken's turn next, and he caught the largest of the trip, a
fish that must have gone four pounds. We released it, and
headed up to camp when Peg and Jim called out that supper

was ready.

For me, the trip was now almost complete. This was our first extended whitewater trip, and we had gained confidence with every set of rapids we ran. We had endured horrendous black flies and mosquitoes, spent time among the Cree at Oxford House, known the satisfaction that accrues after several days on the water. And now we had caught brook trout.

We gathered around the fire to eat supper. The sun went down, and a chill settled over the camp. After humid days with their swarms of bugs, the crisp air felt good. No mosquitoes came out to draw our blood. We made blackberry tea and sat around the fire talking into the night.

Then someone looked up. The northern lights were swirling in the sky. We left the fire and moved to the slanted rock. We sprawled out on our backs, reveling in the 360-degree display above us. The shimmering green waves rose from the horizon to the top of the sky. We cheered every new ghostly shaft as it emerged, but after some time, we just lay there in silence. This show needed no commentary.

We declared the next day a layover day. There would be brook trout for breakfast. And we knew more fish were swimming under the northern lights.

Day at the Office

A gray morning on Manitoba's Seal River. One at a time, my paddling partner David Spencer and I ease into the Old Town Tripper.

With the canoe nudged against the shoreline rocks, we busy ourselves in our respective spray-skirt cockpits as a warm drizzle begins to ooze out of the sky. Midway in a two-week trip, we have slipped into a natural rhythm, and this arranging of our nests in bow and stern is part of it.

We kneel on our kneeling pads, wriggle our legs beneath thigh straps, snug down hat brims, locate paddles, situate cameras, zip life jackets and cinch spray skirts. When we're both settled, we sit quietly while waiting for our four partners to load up.

"Another day in the office," Spencer says.

I know just what he means. We have been doing this for six or seven days now. We have developed a routine that is something like getting up and going to work back home. But out here, there is no monotony to the cycle of daily life on the water. The routine is defined by the simple rhythm of our passage down the river.

Travel on any extended trip revolves around our most basic needs. We take on calories to fuel the day's work. We paddle and portage. We make camp. We take on more calories. We tell a few stories. We sleep.

It's a beautiful existence.

On such a trip, everything falls into place after a few days. You know which packs go in your canoe, which go into your partners' canoes. You can tell the fish breading from the dried eggs in the food pack. You remember where you put the extra batteries for your headlamp.

Everyone in the group knows what needs to be done, and tasks seem to get accomplished almost without effort. Someone rises early and kindles a fire. The coffee pot goes on, along with another for hot water. One by one, others emerge from their tents, assess the day, find their mugs, move toward the fire.

Someone begins rustling in the food pack, and breakfast takes the form of plastic bags set on the dew-laden bottom of an over-turned canoe. It's a regular continental breakfast. Oatmeal. Granola. Dried fruit. Brown sugar. Powdered milk. And, if somebody has been really industrious, maybe some warm blueberry muffins.

Tents come down. Packs are lashed shut. Gear materializes in heaps by the water's edge.

Now our partners are ready. One by one, the canoes push off. We paddle easily for a few minutes, loosening up our muscles. Eventually, we reach the day's cruising speed—three or four miles per hour, depending on how much current is going our way.

Rain dapples my glasses and beads up on the map case. Spencer and I talk sparingly at this hour. We check our maps. We look at the sky. We scan the shoreline for signs of life.

We have no rapids to run for several miles today. The river is flat and quiet. Spencer, in the stern, times his paddle strokes with mine. The canoe moves ahead in little surges that create a gurgle at the bow. I can feel Spencer's stroke behind me. I can see the bow lift slightly each time our paddles bite the water. I could do this forever.

One of the canoes is off to our left a good distance. We would have to shout to be heard. Another is behind, at least as far. Occasionally, two canoes will come side by side, and we'll greet each other.

"Hey."

"Hey."

"Damp, eh?"

"A little bit."

Someone will remark about a feature of the land, or ask about a particular bird's call, or wonder out loud how far ahead the rapids might be. Slowly, without a conscious decision, the canoes drift apart again. Drizzle becomes light rain. We make our miles.

Even in this gray landscape, we know that something remarkable may occur at any moment. A wolf might trot out on a gravel bar and watch our flotilla pass. An Arctic tern might slice past, prospecting the shallows for breakfast. Or we might chance upon a relaxation of seals sprawled on shoreline boulders.

The canoe plows ahead. Water gurgles off the prow. Our paddles swing in time.

It's an excellent office.

RAPIDS TRANSIT

SEEING BUBBLES

In whitewater paddling jargon, surfing a wave is a play move in which a canoe rides a recirculating wave. The canoe points upstream in this move, and if the wave is the right size, the canoe can ride there almost indefinitely with only occasional correcting strokes by the bow and stern paddlers. It takes some work to put the canoe in position on the back-curling wave, but once there, the paddlers can relax though the river is roaring on both sides of them.

Our last morning on the Bloodvein River in 1993, we were camped on a rock overlooking a large recirculating wave. A surfing wave, Ken Gilbertson figured. We had some time on our hands that morning, and none of us was eager to end the trip a few miles downstream at the village of Bloodvein.

"Anyone want to go surf that wave with me?" Gilbertson asked.

I volunteered.

We grabbed our paddles, slipped into our life jackets and took Ken's Old Town Tripper to the river. The plan was to slide down a tongue of fast water, catch an eddy, then work upstream to the curling wave.

Gilbertson is an excellent whitewater paddler—in fact, a whitewater paddling instructor and a veteran northern river traveler. He's a big guy at six-feet-four and over 200 pounds. Which is to say, he always paddles stern. Less experienced as a whitewater paddler and weighing 165 pounds, I paddled the bow.

Once in the eddy, preparing to ferry upstream and catch the wave, Gilbertson made a prediction.

"This is either going to be a lot of fun, or it's going to be over very fast," he said.

The wave, as is typical, looked a lot bigger from the water than it had when we had scouted it from shore. Using short, powerful strokes, we worked upstream until the bow of the canoe found the wave. The river grew very loud. From the bow, I had an intimate view of the river's hydraulics. I could see the tongue of tannin-stained water rushing at us with what appeared to be tremendous speed. It took a serious plunge before it welled up, forming a wave that curled back upstream with more force than we had estimated.

I don't recall us holding our position on the wave for any time at all. No sooner had we arrived in surfing position than the wave sucked us farther upstream. The bow dropped into the trough behind the wave and kept surging upstream. Immediately the rushing tongue of river claimed the bow, pouring over the front deck and filling us up. As the bow augered into the onrushing water, the stern rose sharply.

Gilbertson had been half right. It was over very fast.

The canoe rolled and spit us out. I worked to get out of the thigh straps that we use to hold us in a secure paddling position. Then I was free of the canoe and drifting downstream, completely underwater. I opened my eyes and saw nothing but amber bubbles rising in front of me. I held onto my paddle, and the river delivered me to the surface. Gilbertson was floating just downstream of me. We grabbed the canoe, which was wallowing next to us, and rode out the short rapid. The water was warm, so there was no urgency in getting to shore.

Our four companions had all been watching this unfold from camp. We knew they must have gotten a kick out of our folly. Now they were on the rocks at an eddy below camp, waiting to help us wade ashore and empty the canoe.

There are plenty of ways to get humbled on a wild river, and this is just one of them. In this case, our liabilities were low. We had attempted our surfing move in an empty canoe, with no food or gear to lose. The water was warm, and the rapid was short. We didn't have to worry about getting cold, and we knew we could easily swim to shore just below camp.

In the past twenty years of paddling northern rivers, we've had only a few swamping episodes, all of them benign. Phyllis and I dumped on the Gods River in northern Manitoba on our first northern trip. But again, we were empty. We had stopped to play and practice for a few hours in the first small set of rapids on the Gods. As whitewater paddlers, we were rookies then, and we were practicing all the moves we might need later on the river—eddying out, peeling out of an eddy, forward ferrying, back ferrying. We had done several successful back ferries. Next thing we knew, we were swimming.

That's how it almost always happens. Quickly. One moment you're right side up. The next, you're down there with the bubbles. We weren't the only ones who swam in that practice session, but the practice paid off. All of our canoes stayed right-side up in the next two weeks on our trip down the Gods to Hudson Bay.

The most memorable swamping I've ever been part of occurred not on a canoe trip, but on a day's rafting trip down the St. Louis River near Duluth. A local rafting company had put together a trip with several four-person rafts. Most of the paddlers were from the Minneapolis-St. Paul area, and many of them had little paddling experience. The St. Louis River is a relatively easygoing river in summer months, and water levels were not especially high on this day.

We approached a drop called Electric Ledge, so-named because it makes a quick drop under a set of power lines. It's about a six-foot descent, not a sheer drop but a good ride nonetheless. We got out to scout the drop, then hopped back in our rafts to make the plunge. I had run Electric Ledge a few times before in canoes, always successfully, and I wasn't especially concerned about our fate in the raft.

Like a rubber ducky, our raft slid toward the ledge. We paddled steadily to hold our line, but something went wrong. We slid into the drop, and the rest of the run felt as if we were in the bottom of a toilet in midflush. All of us popped out of the raft and quickly surfaced. But some of us were a little more shaken than others. What I recall most vividly is a woman shrieking for her husband.

"Frank! Frank! Frank!" she cried.

I tried to calm her. I could see Frank. He had found a rock at midstream and seemed intent on digging his fingernails into it. He wasn't planning to leave that rock anytime soon.

Frank's wife finally saw that he was going to live, and we walked her to shore while we reclaimed the raft. The only task left was to pry Frank off the rock so we could continue downstream. We managed to accomplish that without the use of crowbars or ropes and continued on downstream, back in the raft.

We don't mind the occasional swamping on the St. Louis River, where we make our training runs. We carry no gear on these day trips, so there's no serious consequence to a swim. The farther we get from home on our northern trips, though, the more conservative we get in big water. We really like dry sleeping bags and dry food packs.

We've had a few spills among our crews in the past twenty years on those trips, but none of them produced any serious situations. We once managed to lodge an Old Town Tripper on pyramid-shaped rock at midstream on Manitoba's Poplar River. As if in slow motion, the two paddlers realized the canoe wasn't going to budge, and the river began to flow among the packs in the bottom of the canoe. The two paddlers climbed out, and we all watched the river fold the boat around the rock.

It wasn't a pretty sight. And none of us wanted to try to squeeze six paddlers and their gear into two canoes for the rest of the trip. We didn't have to. The Poplar River was shallow in these rapids. Several of us worked together to dislodge the canoe. Once off the rock, the remarkable Royalex boat snapped back into its original shape. We dumped the water out of it, reloaded the packs and we were good to go again.

Amazing? Not really. That's why we use Trippers, made with Old Town's Royalex construction. Royalex is unbelievably tough. You can scratch its outer layer of plastic on sharp rocks, but it's nearly impossible to puncture a Tripper. The Royalex material also slides off most rocks, a valued attribute when you're paddling shallow, boulder-field whitewater.

The only time we've seen a Tripper slit completely through was when a polar bear jumped on it while we were camped at the mouth of Manitoba's Seal River in 1998. We didn't see the polar bear jumping on our three overturned Trippers. We just heard it. But the next day, paddling along the shore of Hudson Bay, Dick Adams and Dan Theis noticed they were taking on a little water. Back on shore, they discovered a long slit in the bottom of the canoe. Fortunately, we were just waiting for a boat pick-up from Churchill, so we didn't have to paddle unless we wanted to poke around among the beluga whales.

We use Trippers against the possibility of things going awry, but we work hard not to put ourselves into a position where we really have to appreciate them.

DIVE LEFT!

It wasn't one of our better moments. The canoe was pointing upstream, but we were headed downstream in a frisky set of rapids on Ontario's Pipestone River.

Dave Spencer shouted at me from the stern.

"You mind just finishing this one out backwards?" he yelled.

I have no idea what I yelled back, but that's exactly what we did. We bounced down that bony rapids stern-first, salvaging an ugly run. It isn't easy running rapids looking over your shoulder, but it's possible.

When we reached the pool at the bottom, we re-oriented ourselves with the river and paddled on downstream as if nothing had happened.

If you run enough rivers, you're going to find yourself a little turned around once in a while. Just when you get to thinking you and your partner are a pretty accomplished whitewater tandem, a river slaps you around and helps you rediscover your humility. The trick is reacquiring your humility without losing the food pack.

When you're running whitewater well, when you seem to be in perfect synchronicity with your paddling partner, it's like being in "the zone" athletes often talk about. The river seems almost to slow down. Every move comes naturally. You draw. Your partner in the stern draws. The canoe slides laterally across the current. You find the next slot of current, avoid a boulder, take splash over the bow, ride out the standing waves and eddy out to watch your fellow paddlers negotiate the run.

The fact that you're a thousand miles or so from home, with all your essential possessions in the canoe, only makes the experience sweeter.

In twenty years of river tripping, our little clan has had no serious unplanned swims. Oh, someone manages to fill a canoe now and then. And there was that time a couple of us wrapped an Old Town Tripper spine-first around a rock on the Poplar River, but in every case, we've come out unscathed. No canoes disabled. No long, cold swims. No gear lost except the occasional fishing rod.

One morning on the Winisk River, which flows to Hudson Bay in northern Ontario, Spencer and I found ourselves one set of rapids out of sync with those on our maps. We rounded a wide bend in the river and saw what appeared to be a formidable stretch of whitewater. This was Bearhead Rapids, which scouting reports had told us to run on river right, then portage at the lower end. But we didn't think we were in Bearhead Rapids. We thought we were still one rapids upstream.

"Wanna pull over and scout?" I hollered.

"No. Let's just stay river left," Spencer replied.

The farther we moved downstream, the less "left" there was. Soon enough, we found ourselves dancing a tight line between some large and unfriendly waves on our right and some large and unfriendly rocks on our left. Avoiding the waves, we inadvertently put the Tripper smack on a pointy boulder, where we began to rotate like a needle in a compass.

We had paddled enough whitewater together that we didn't

The author (center) in 1964 on his first trip to the Quetico-Superior canoe country along the Minnesota–Ontario border as an Explorer Scout. He was 15 at the time. The experience spawned a lifetime of canoe trips. (photo by John Stone)

Ken Gilbertson (Duluth, Minnesota) shows how we'll make an upstream ferry in the fog on Manitoba's Gods River. [*Learning on the Fly*] (This photo and all following photos by Sam Cook)

Slices of a spruce tree helped us fashion makeshift oarlock supports for a raft before we started down Alaska's Tana River. The oarlock supports were forgotten at home. [*Some Assembly Required*]

Churning glacial waters on the Tana River in Wrangell-St. Elias National Park and Preserve in Alaska. Perry Webster of Duluth, Minnesota mans the oars. [*Some Assembly Required*]

Low

The two-mile Bayly Portage from Bayly Lake to Gods Lake in northern Manitoba was a good workout. Most of it was through a soggy bog. Jim Suttie of Duluth, Minnesota tried dragging his canoe rather than carrying it. [*The Longest Carry*]

The unexpected happens when you least expect it! A black wolf walked into camp one afternoon on the Mountain River in the Northwest Territories.

It took us quite a while to find this tiny tributary at the headwaters of the Mountain River in the Northwest Territories. And once we found it, it was too small to paddle. [*A Good River is Hard to Find*]

We ate breakfast in the rain at a marginal campsite on Manitoba's Bloodvein River. As on most trips, things were about to get better. [*Highs and Lows on the Bloodvein*]

Early morning company. A black bear swims across the river at sunrise on Manitoba's Pigeon River. [*Life is Good*]

Dave Baumgarten of Duluth, Minnesota steam-dries his fleece pants after a damp day on Manitoba's Seal River. [*Life is Good*]

Paddlers unload canoes on a black-sand beach above the Fifth Canyon of the Mountain River. The Mountain River flows down through the Mackenzie Mountains of Canada's Northwest Territories to the Mackenzie River. [*Off the Beaten Path*]

The author's wife, Phyllis, holds a brook trout caught at No Name Falls on the Gods River in 1983. Several brook trout of that size were caught in the fast water below the falls. [*Brookies for Breakfast*]

A lone paddler makes a crossing to an offshore island at Pukaskwa National Park on Lake Superior in Ontario. [*Pukaskwa Passage*]

Dave Spencer (Duluth, Minnesota) and Dave Baumgarten take a break on the clear waters of Lake Superior at Ontario's Pukaskwa National Park. [*Pukaskwa Passage*]

A paddler unloads his canoe at camp in a cove along
Lake Superior in Ontario's Pukaskwa National Park.
[*Pukaskwa Passage*]

It was a team effort as we slid and lined our loaded Old
Town Tripper over a ledge on the Bloodvein River.

Dave Spencer (bow) and Ken Gilbertson drop into a tongue of
whitewater on the Bloodvein River in Manitoba.

With paddlers listening hard for the sound of rapids, a couple of canoes
venture into the fog on Manitoba's Seal River. [*Day at the Office*]

The father-son team of Seth Spencer (bow) and David Spencer run an empty canoe through rapids on Manitoba's Bloodvein River.

Jeff Bassett (in kayak) prepares to rescue Kathleen Rennan of Duluth, Minnesota after she bounced out of the raft in a difficult stretch of rapids on Alaska's Tana River. [*Trial on the Tana*]

Camps look small along the Nigu River in Alaska's sprawling
Brooks Range. [*High Arctic Odyssey*]

We're never the first folks to pass this way. Mike Reitz of
Fairbanks, Alaska, stands next to a rock ring along the Nigu
River. The stones are thought to be part of a structure used
by native people who hunted in the area. [*High Arctic Odyssey*]

Two barren grounds caribou run across a high plateau along the
Nigu River in Alaska's Brooks Range. [*High Arctic Odyssey*]

It's not all paddling. Hikers head for the hills in the shadow of the Brooks Range after making camp. The tundra was already turning colors. [*High Arctic Odyssey*]

At the end of our trip on the Seal River, we stayed in this plywood shack on Hudson Bay. A polar bear approached the shack the first night we were there. [*King of the Coast*]

A polar bear left its track in the soft mud along Hudson Bay after he paid a visit during the night. Dave Baumgarten of Duluth had fired one warning shot from his shotgun to discourage the bear from approaching any closer. [*King of the Coast*]

The author caught this 44-inch northern pike ("jackfish" in Canada) during a rest break on the Poplar River in Manitoba. The fish was released. [*Jackfish, eh?*]

Freshwater relative of the salmon. Arctic grayling inhabit rivers in Canada and Alaska. Dan Theis of Duluth caught it on a fly on Manitoba's Seal River. [*Jackfish, eh?*]

Miklos Jalics of Budapest, Hungary, shows off the makings of fish chowder on the Bloodvein River—a northern pike, a channel catfish and some walleyes. [*Jackfish, eh?*]

Dan Theis (Duluth, Minnesota) fly-fishes for Arctic grayling on Willow Handle Lake, near the headwaters of the Mountain River in Canada's Northwest Territories.

David Spencer and friends take a break in the Ojibwa village of Webequie on Ontario's Winisk River. [*Extortion on the Winisk*]

We purchased these gauntlet mittens and moccasins from women in the Ojibwa village of Webequie on the Winisk River in northern Ontario. [*Extortion on the Winisk*]

Dan Theis (from left), Dave Baumgarten and Dick Adams (Superior, Wisconsin) help unload our canoes from a Twin Otter on Stoney Lake in northern Manitoba, our put-in for paddling the Seal River. [*Saying Goodbye to a River*]

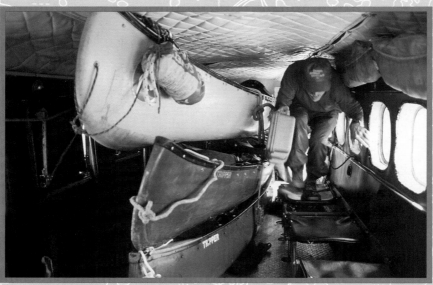

Dick Adams makes his way through the coach section of a well-loaded Twin Otter on our way to the Seal River. [*Saying Goodbye to a River*]

Fireweed flourishes after a fire along an esker on the Seal River in northern Manitoba. [*Mason Camp*]

Caribou antlers littered the eskers along the Seal River. One resides in the author's garden bringing back canoe trip memories. [*Mason Camp*]

This plaque is mounted on a stone-and-mortar memorial to Canadian paddler, author and filmmaker Bill Mason on Manitoba's Seal River. [*Mason Camp*]

Notes on maps are not only references for future trips but also rekindle memories. [*Bringing it Back*]

A large thunderhead dominates the sunset on Windigo Lake, our take-out point after paddling Manitoba's Pigeon River.

Late evening sunlight bathes the hills along the Nigu River in the Brooks Range of northern Alaska.

The Poplar River in Manitoba swirls around a midstream rock, carrying the evening clouds with it.

Early in the trip, we have the luxury of eating fresh food. We enjoyed this chicken stir-fry meal the first night of our Steel River trip in Ontario.

Sometimes your body tells you it wants fat. On the cold Chitina River in Alaska, Dave Spencer built lunch (from the bottom up) with an Oreo cookie, cream cheese, peanut butter and canned turkey.

Thick black flies and mosquitoes necessitate the technique of eating breakfast while wearing a headnet. Dave Baumgarten on the Seal River of Manitoba.

Scourge of the North...or at least one of them. Mosquitoes cling to a paddler's back. Bugs like these require one to use the eating technique shown above.

Mist and fog hangs over a small rapids on Manitoba's Bloodvein River, a tributary of Lake Winnipeg.

This is what it's all about. David Spencer runs a tongue of whitewater solo in an empty canoe on Manitoba's Bloodvein River.

On a cold and misty morning
on the Seal River, Dan Theis
and Dick Adams find a quiet
slot in a set of rapids.

When a set of rapids proves
too big to run, sometimes we
slide or line the canoes
through a smaller chute off
the main channel. This is the
Bloodvein River in Manitoba.

Gods Lake, Manitoba

panic. We kept leaning downstream, performing our little pirouette, until finally we slid off the rock. Surprisingly, we were both facing downstream, just they way they teach you in the books and videos.

One challenge remained. We saw a ledge ahead and a foamy hole below it. Foamy holes are to be avoided because the water there, full of bubbles, is more air than liquid. Air doesn't float a canoe well, and canoes tend to ride low, then take on water and sometimes capsize.

But we had no choice. Our one hope was to hit the hole with enough momentum to carry us out of it and downriver.

"Punch it!" Spencer yelled.

We careened off the lip of the ledge and stalled momentarily in the hole. I reached ahead, trying to grab some solid water, and somehow we inched out of the hole. Now the river widened and flattened. We had made it.

We always feel a little sheepish when we've escaped imminent disaster. We felt a little more sheepish when we realized that we had been running Bearhead Rapids inadvertently.

That moment seemed only a mild miscue, though, compared to a rapids we encountered on the Mountain River. Six of us were running the powerful current of the Third Canyon on that cold Northwest Territories river. We weren't far below the Arctic Circle—the Mountain flows into the Mackenzie River, which flows north to the Arctic Ocean.

The canyon walls towered over us as we approached a long set of rapids. We pulled over on a gravel bar at river left to get a look at what lay ahead. Mike DeBevec of Grand Marais and I walked as far down the bar as we could to scout. It appeared the river tapered from right to left in a series of curling waves nobody would want to see up close. We agreed that a slot on river left offered a skinny but safe passage where the waves ended.

Spencer and I pushed off first. The voice of the river grew louder and louder as the waves angled toward the canyon wall. We rode smooth current cautiously toward the slot, but as we got closer, we could see that something didn't look right. Instead of a smooth passage, we could see we were in for a wild ride. The river poured over the lip of a ledge in a powerful black tongue and piled up on itself in a series of standing waves. There was no turning back, with all of the river's current pushing toward our side of the river, up against the canyon wall.

"We're in it!" Spencer shouted as we committed to the drop.

The bow plunged down the face of the tongue in what must have been a four-foot drop. The river rose up again, heaving itself into the curling waves. We were paddling a canoe with spray skirts, which would have kept some of the water out. But those waves were no place to spend any quality time.

"Dive left!" I heard Spencer yell.

Go ahead and look in all of the paddling guides you can find. You won't find the term "Dive left!" anywhere. But it seemed a prudent course of action.

I tried to pry the bow to the left as we skimmed the edge of the first big wave. There wasn't much room between the wave train and the canyon wall on our left. Spencer drew his end of the canoe left, too, and we powered ahead, picking our way between the waves and the sheer rock wall. Finally, the river widened, and we eddied out on river left behind a small cleft in the canyon wall.

The others had been watching us from the gravel bar. They couldn't tell exactly what we had discovered, and there was no way we could tell them. They would find out soon enough themselves. We held our position, ready to initiate a rescue if either of the other canoes had a mishap.

They all dived left, too, and drove past us looking for eddies of their own.

TRIAL ON THE TANA

We had had plenty of time to survey this set of rapids on Alaska's Tana River. Our camp the night before had been perched on a bench overlooking the run. As we pitched tents, as we prepared supper, as we wrote in our journals, we couldn't help assessing this lively piece of water.

The Tana River rises from the base of the Tana Glacier in Alaska's Wrangell-St. Elias National Park and Preserve. Thick with its payload of glacial silt, the river runs an opaque gray on the way to its confluence with the Chitina River. Like the glacier from which it originates, it also runs ice cold, just a few degrees above freezing on this July morning.

Fourteen of us had signed on for this exploratory raft trip down thirty miles of the Tana and another seventy on the Chitina. The University of Minnesota Duluth Outdoor Program had sponsored the trip. We knew roughly what we had taken on. The Tana is a seldom-run river, and trip leader Randy Carlson of UMD told us we would likely be the only group to run the river that summer of 1995.

The Tana offered rapids up to Class IV on the I-through-VI international whitewater scale. In other words, it was big water in a remote wilderness setting.

Carlson had gathered us in camp early in the trip, before we even reached the river, for a safety briefing.

"What we're looking at is a no-swim scenario," Carlson had

said, among other things. "If it's a swim situation, we would see that as a breakdown. We're not out to run the most difficult whitewater we've ever done and be heroes."

Now it was our second day on the river, and we were ready to tackle this 300-yard rapids just off our camp. We had scouted it from shore and the raft captains—Carlson, Duluth's David Spencer and Duluth's Perry Webster—each had a route chosen. Preceding the three rafts down the river would be kayakers Jim Morrison of Duluth and Jeff Bassett of Anchorage.

The kayaks offered an added element of safety. Morrison and Bassett, experienced whitewater paddlers, would precede us down a stretch of whitewater, then signal, using paddles, where they wanted the rafts to go. In the event someone did come out of a raft, the kayakers would be close by for a timely rescue.

The Tana was perhaps 100 yards wide at this point, bucking and churning in a series of standing waves. Carlson and his four passengers—all wearing long underwear, helmets, drysuits or neoprene wetsuits—shoved off and let the current take them. Carlson, an expert rafter and veteran of many western river trips, angled the raft into the current and set a course down the middle of the river. The rest of us watched and took pictures from shore.

The ride was spirited even for a heavily loaded fourteen-foot raft. Bassett and Morrison waited in an eddy near the base of the rapids. Everything was going smoothly until the raft caught a huge hole—a large, recirculating hydraulic that holds whatever happens into it. The raft was caught and thrown high but not flipped.

Duluth's Kathleen Rennan, riding up front in the raft,

described the moment.

"I was looking directly into a sheet of water," Rennan said in camp that night. "The top was far above my head. The boat started up, but the wave rose over the top of the boat. When the wave hit me, I flew to the left, upstream and flew out into the water. I started somersaulting."

Everyone else managed to stay in the raft. Meanwhile, Rennan was in the icy water, under the raft. She managed to come free and popped to the surface in the fast current. Those of us watching on shore were relieved to see her yellow life jacket amid the chaos of gray water. But her troubles weren't over.

"I saw the raft hadn't tipped," said Rennan, who was making her first raft trip. "But I was quite a ways downstream."

She saw Bassett in his kayak, paddling furiously to reach her, already fifty yards downstream from the raft.

"I thought, 'I can't drown. I have two children,'" Rennan said. "My eyes were scratchy with the silt. I started to cry when I saw Jeff coming, when I saw I had a rescue."

It took little encouragement from Bassett for Rennan to grab him around the waist and drape herself over the back of his kayak. Then Bassett began digging for shore.

"He asked me, 'Are you okay?' I kept saying, 'I'm so cold. I'm so cold. I'm so cold.' It was so scary," Rennan said.

Bassett reached an eddy, and Rennan was safe. Cold but safe.

Meanwhile, Carlson and his passengers had shifted enough of their weight to the front of the raft so that it eventually worked free of the hydraulic. Shaken but intact, they rode out the rest of the fast water and tucked into the eddy with Rennan and the kayakers.

Spencer and Webster chose to steer their rafts far to river right, hugging the boulders along shore and avoiding the hole that had grabbed Carlson's raft. We all gathered on shore downstream and had another chat about river safety.

In retrospect, after the initial incident, everything had gone well. Rennan kept her composure. Bassett made the rescue he had practiced countless times. Carlson and his remaining passengers kept their raft upright. Nevertheless, it was sobering moment for all fourteen of us. We were a long way from civilization, and we had only each other to rely on.

We made the rest of the trip without incident. That night in camp, Carlson offered Rennan a symbolic treat.

"Kathleen, you get a piece of licorice," he said, "for getting back in the raft."

RUNNING IT RIGHT

Early evening on Ontario's Pipestone River. It's our first day out on a trip that will take Dave Spencer and I down the Pipestone and a good way down the Winisk River toward Hudson Bay.

As the sunlight slants across the river, we survey a set of rapids before us. Already, we've run several sets and made one half-mile portage. The top end of this drop looks runnable on river left. We'll have some rocks to avoid but enough water to get us where we're going. From there, we can't tell. The river makes a sweeping bend to the right. We'll have to figure the rest out as we go.

Our margin of error is thin on this trip. Through a combination of unusual factors, we have found ourselves on the river alone. On most trips, our group totals four or six or eight, giving us a greater cushion of safety should something happen.

We had planned this trip for four, but that changed the night before we left. So, we decided to forge on with just the two of us. That meant a more careful consideration of the risks we would take, but we accepted that.

Now the canoe approached the lip of the rapids. In the bow, I had snugged my spray skirt around my waist. I felt a mild wave of anticipation, the way I always feel at the top of a run. It's the same feeling you get on a rock cliff just before you decide to leap into the still waters ten or twenty feet below. All of your senses seem to open up. Time turns elastic. You are infused with equal parts thrill and fear.

This is what you have come for.

Now strands of smooth river slide over a small ledge, and the run begins. The canoe begins to buck and heave. The bow plunges into a wave trough, and a curl of tannin-stained river smacks my chest. Now the bow rises again and the river seems far below.

Over the tumult of the river, Spencer calls out our course.

"Left of the dark rock."

"Right of the pointed rock."

"Eddy out behind the big rock."

Eddying out in a lively river is one of the sweetest moves a pair of canoeists can make. Spencer angles the canoe across the eddy line between the fast current and the slack water behind the rock. As soon as the bow bites the slack water, I plant a high brace. That holds the bow in the quiet water, facing upstream, while the current swings the stern downstream. When Spencer's end of the canoe hits the slow water, we each give a couple of quick forward strokes to snug the bow up to the rock.

We're there, lolling in this backwater below the rock. The river rips past us on both sides, but in this sliver of an eddy, we can rest. The eddy, pushing upstream, holds us near the rock with little effort on our part.

We have learned to seek out these bits of respite in challenging rapids. From here, we can look over our shoulders and decide upon our next move.

Spencer and I can see what we need to do here. We need to move from river left, where we started these rapids, to far river right. There are too many exposed boulders in this garden of rocks to continue on our original course.

Spencer has a plan. Still facing upstream, we plan to move across the river to another eddy, and, if that proves successful, repeat the move to yet another eddy. These moves are called ferries, in this case, upstream ferries.

The challenge is this: We cannot afford to drop downstream as we make these lateral moves. The river is studded with rocks. If we let the current catch us and turn us broadside, we'll founder on those rocks. What would happen next is hard to say, but none of the options is fun to think about. We'll have to be crisp in our moves, drawing the bow just enough into the current so that Spencer can hold the angle as we slide over to the next eddy. It isn't far, but we'll be crossing a lively jet of river.

"Ready?" Spencer shouts.

I nod.

"Draw left."

I reach out on the left and pull the paddle directly back to the canoe. The bow catches the fast water. Once the angle is set, I paddle ahead briskly. Spencer holds the angle perfectly. Five, six, seven strokes. Boom. We're in the next eddy. Just that easy.

"One more time?" he yells.

I can see the next eddy. Here we go.

I draw the bow into the jet of fast water. The angle is just right. We hold our position and let the river slide us into the next eddy. Perfect. We're there.

The light is golden. The river froths around us. We are wet and young and strong, and there is no place in the world we would rather be.

Still facing upstream, we look back over our shoulders to check out the rest of the run. It's a clear shot all the way on river right. A train of waves dances at the runout, but we'll just skirt that on the right to avoid shipping any water.

We push the bow across the eddy line and catch the current. I lean downstream. Spencer keeps driving the canoe until the stern is free of the eddy. We're rocking and rolling now, headed downstream. Now we're jostling alongside the wave train. We've made it.

The river opens up again and lies flat. We take just a second to look back upstream, savoring our clean run. It gets up inside of you, a run like that. Executing your strokes. Working in tandem with your partner. Taking what the river gives you. Arriving safe and relatively dry at the bottom.

If you think we ever tire of this, you are mistaken.

Now, we turn downstream again and paddle into the evening light. It's time to find a camp.

UNEXPECTED ENCOUNTERS

HIGH ARCTIC ODYSSEY

L aura wants to see a grizzly. She reminds one of our guides, Mike Reitz, of this at least once a day. "Mike, I want to see a grizzly," she says.

Laura is from California. She has never seen a grizzly. She and her husband, Eric, and I are the only paying customers on a twelve-day trip down the remote Nigu River starting in Alaska's Gates of the Arctic National Park and Preserve.

I quietly cringe every time Laura announces her grizzly quest. I'd like to see a bear, too. But it seems a bit bold, karma-wise, to want it so badly and announce it so often. In the Alaskan wilderness, it seems wise to take things as they come rather than trying to write your own script.

You want a grizzly too much and it might poke its nose through your tent to say hello.

This is the tenth day of our trip, August 17, 2003. Forty-six degrees. A steady rain has dogged us for much of the trip and taps on our tents this morning. The weather seems inclement to me, but guides Ramona Finnoff and Reitz can't get over how balmy this trip is for mid-August.

"Amazingly warm," Reitz says at breakfast, in the shelter of the cook tent. "No frost. No snow."

It can snow every month of the year in Gates of the Arctic. We are 150 miles north of the Arctic Circle, in the heart of Alaska's Brooks Range.

This is a remarkable place to wake up every morning. The Nigu serpentines through a broad valley flanked by peaks that rise to nearly 4,000 feet. Great green swatches of tundra roll up the peaks. All of these mountains have been glaciated, their peaks scoured and softened under the press of ice.

Climb one of the hundreds of unnamed mountains here, and you can see for miles. Look upstream and see where you've been for the past several days. Look downstream into your next day's itinerary. In the distant haze lie land-locked lakes. You can hike and climb for hours and look down upon your tent, a dot of color along the river.

Numbers can't begin to convey the sense of scale in this place. Gates of the Arctic encompasses seven million acres of wilderness. If it were a state, seven other states would be smaller.

Despite the 35-degree rains we have awoken to on several days and the sheer immensity of the land, I have felt comfortable here from the moment our floatplane touched down. John Kauffman, a National Park Service planner, once wrote of this landscape:

> The strange beauty of the Gates of the Arctic country is not easily described, nor are its effects upon the human spirit. The land seems forbidding at first; but as the body toughens and spirits rise, time stops, space expands, humility and confidence grow together.

We saw another outfitted group at our put-in lake, near the continental divide, ten days ago. We departed on the Nigu before them, and we will not see them again.

The river is fast but benign. Unlike many other northern canoe trips my companions and I have made, where whitewater is part of the experience, the Nigu is quick but smooth. As much as anything, it is an artery that allows us to move through the land, exploring as we go.

After a leisurely breakfast, we pack up in a light rain and move downstream. Today, I give Eric the "rubber ducky," a yellow inflatable kayak. I paddle bow with Reitz in one of our two Ally Pak canoes. As their name implies, Ally Paks come in bags. At our headwaters lake, we assembled their interlocking aluminum frames inside a tough vinyl skin. Rigid but flexible, they have carried Finnoff and Reitz hundreds of miles down Alaskan rivers.

Laura is in luck. During the morning paddle, we come upon a bear. The barren-ground grizzly is feeding along a broad tundra plain about 300 yards away. It's an adult, blondish brown. It has no idea we exist.

Bears need a lot of room up here. A barren-ground grizzly's territory ranges from 60 to 100 square miles. He, or she, might cover eight miles a day, excavating Arctic ground squirrels from the tundra or grazing on vegetation. We watch the bear until it swaggers over a rise.

Laura is happy. She would be even happier by the time we make camp that evening. We see two more grizzlies during the day—another perhaps a mile away as we eat lunch, and a third feasting on blueberries as we paddle past.

Even at a distance, the bears are impressive. They are huge and thick. Their brown fur seems to flow over their muscles as they pad deliberately along. They walk as if they own the place.

Finnoff and Reitz have been close to bears a number of times without serious incident. On one trip, a grizzly walked into Finnoff's group camp. Every member of the group was in tents, reading or resting, except one man, who was out for a walk. The bear lumbered over to that man's tent, leaped into the air and landed on the tent, crushing it, Finnoff said. Then it walked away.

At midafternoon, we pull over to inspect a spot where the land has slumped toward the river, revealing a cross-section of tundra and permafrost. We are on a hillside above the river when we see a file of about twenty caribou moving along the far side, perhaps two hundred yards away. Reitz assumes a caribou impersonation, raising his arms over his head as if to infer antlers, then rocking side to side. Because caribou are herding animals, he says, they can sometimes be persuaded to join another caribou, even if he's wearing orange rain pants and a blue life jacket.

The caribou keep coming our way, led by an old cow with two calves. They drop into the river, ford it without apparent effort, climb out on our side and trot up the rise not twenty yards away. We can feel their footfalls. We can hear them breathing.

They are part of the Western Arctic caribou herd, some 500,000 strong, that migrates over the Brooks Range twice a year. In the spring, they move north to their calving grounds on the coast of the Arctic Ocean. This time of year, they are just beginning to move south again, to their wintering grounds on the south side of the range. Wolves follow, taking stragglers and wayward calves.

It is a privilege to be traveling in one of the world's last vast ecosystems, where caribou and grizzlies and wolves still interact as they have for thousands of years. Native people have followed and hunted these caribou through the eons. What is our twelve-day passage against that throw of time?

We make camp that night at 6:00 P.M., but supper is not on the agenda just yet. In an hour, we are laboring through wet tussocks and then dry tundra to reach a pass several hundred feet above us. We do this every day, either before or after paddling. The climbing is addicting. Every bench, every plateau, every scree-laden slope, affords another spectacular vista.

Already, the day is beyond expectation—the bears, the caribou swimming the river before us. But in this land of midnight sun, it seems unacceptable to waste even an hour of light. The rain has ceased. We are nearing a pass below a 3,370-foot peak when Reitz, up ahead, turns toward me and the others. His thumbs touch the sides of his head. His fingers are outstretched above. We know what that means. Caribou ahead.

He has seen only the antlers. With my camera and modest telephoto lens, I scurry to the lip of the plateau. When I pop over, I see two magnificent bulls at rest. When they see me, they clamber to their feet and begin trotting to my left. I am perhaps forty yards from them. They seem to float over the dry tundra, hardly touching the ground as they run. They hold their muzzles high in that characteristic caribou way, which only adds to their appearance of defying gravity.

Now the bulls are describing a great arc about me, dropping down the ridge we have just hiked up. They circle around Mike and Ramona and Eric and Laura, dropping out of my sight. Now Mike is waving frantically at me to be ready. The caribou are making a complete circle and will soon pass by me again. I cannot see them until they pop up onto the plateau, gobbling up the terrain in an easy gait.

Light is fading now, and we are in the shadow of the mountain, but I keep making photos, hoping for the best. After completing the circle, the bulls drop over the other side of the pass and disappear around the mountain.

I cannot speak for the others, but I am awestruck, humbled and grateful to have shared this small piece of the planet with those bulls for a few fleeting seconds. The photo graces my living room wall.

I return to Gates of the Arctic every day.

PUKASKWA PASSAGE

This is how clear Lake Superior is off the shores of Ontario's Pukaskwa ("PUK-uh-saw") National Park. As we paddle along the granite outcrops of the Canadian Shield shoreline, we see a band of darker rock snaking through the lighter granite.

This blackish intrusion of rock rises and falls along the shoreline until we come to a bay. The intrusion drops to the water's edge. In our three canoes, the six of us dawdle along, following the dark band of rock across the lake bottom—twenty, thirty, forty feet below. Now the band of rock is rising again as we reach the other side of the bay. Here it comes—up, up, up.

And there it is on shore again, still folded into the granite, rising over the next point of land.

In a week along this fifty-mile wilderness shoreline, we watch this happen time and again. So transparent is the water that we spend most of our paddling time near shore, heads hung over the gunwales, bottom-watching. We trace giant cracks in the lake's rocky bed. We follow white veins in dark bedrock. We see underwater bays full of bowling-ball boulders. We paddle over shallow bays of sand corrugated by wind and wave action.

Most of us live near another shore of Lake Superior at Duluth, far to the south. But here on the Pukaskwa shoreline, this is a much different Lake Superior. For one, the highway that circumscribes the lake runs fifty miles inland around the park. That means you can paddle the shoreline here without seeing, or even hearing, a truck downshifting among the hills.

Then, too, the water hardly warms up during the summer. During our July trip, the warmest water we find is 48 degrees.

The Canadians knew what they had in this rugged and wild shoreline, and the government designated it a National Park in 1983. The only access to the full sweep of the coastline is by boat or canoe, or by backpack over a hiking trail that follows the shoreline.

We had ridden Bruce McCuaig's tugboat down the shore and plopped our canoes into the water near the Pukaskwa River. For six days, we would paddle and poke our way north to park headquarters at Hattie Cove near Marathon, Ontario.

We paddle spray-covered canoes out of respect for the big lake. Other Pukaskwa travelers prefer sea kayaks, motorboats or sailboats. It's a big piece of water. Paddling northwest, you look over your left shoulder and realize there's nothing but open water for three hundred miles back to Duluth. It makes you want to pay attention.

Our first morning on the water, we notice something in the water between Richardson Island and the mainland. A bear? A moose?

When it reaches shore, it climbs out of the water and looks over its shoulder at us. It's a woodland caribou. The park supports a small population of these once-numerous animals. We feel lucky to have seen one.

The caribou turns away from us, rocks back on its haunches slightly, then lurches forward and trots around the point.

We camp that evening on a small sand beach next to the mouth of the Cascade River. The river splits into three branches on a rocky promontory above the lake. All three branches of the river cascade directly into the lake, one of the few places that happens around the entire lake.

Tom Bell and I pitch our tent on the sand. As we drop off to sleep that night, out one door of the tent we can see the Cascade River dropping into Lake Superior. Out the other, a half-moon is rising over a serrated ridge of spruce.

That camp was just one of several idyllic camps we would make along the Pukaskwa shoreline. We would rise early, make our miles, then tuck into a protected bay to camp. All of these bays—Oiseau, White Spruce Harbor, Fish Harbor, Picture Island Harbor—were well protected from the open lake by bulwarks of rock. We make our camps early in the day and spend the day exploring on foot.

Sometimes we would hop onto the Coastal Hiking Trail, which runs most of the length of the park, and hike to another bay. Or we would just clamber over rocks and hike to the next incoming river to fish or swim. The immense scale of the Pukaskwa coast amazed us daily. We walked along beaches and coves full of driftwood. These were entire bleached trees, piled like pick-up sticks. We stand on these beaches trying to imagine the waves that heaved those trees ashore.

We discover the well-known "Pukaskwa Pits," depressions in the cobblestone beaches well above current lake levels. It is clear by the lichen growing on the cobblestones that these pits have been there for a long time. The pits are one to three feet deep, most of them large enough to hold a couple of people. Nobody knows what they might have been used for.

It's good to know some mystery remains in the world.

The pits are just one feature of the Pukaskwa shoreline that makes the place so spectacular. The geology of the shore is like nothing any of us has seen at our end of the lake. Offshore rock islands appear to have oozed into place like lava. Rounded and wave-swept, some are barren of vegetation. From others, spruce trees appear to grow out of solid rock.

Some shoreline rocks, especially in Oiseau Bay, look like swirls of maple and caramel laced with bands of metallic-flecked licorice. In places, sheer cliffs line the shore. If there is any chop on the lake, we paddle with the constant sound of waves chewing at the rocks and cliffs.

For five days, we enjoy near-perfect weather. Mostly calm seas. Warm days. Little fog. We had built extra time into our schedule. Park officials caution that paddlers can expect to be windbound three days out of ten on the Pukaskwa shoreline.

Our final morning, we awaken to a dense overcast and the sound of treetops tossing in the wind. We eat our breakfast quickly and without much conversation. We have only a couple of miles to go that morning to reach Hattie Cove, but a good portion of the distance would be rounding Campbell Point, a long peninsula of rock that juts into the lake. It offers no safe harbors and no chances of good landings.

Once out of the protection of the Picture Islands, we are greeted with three-foot seas. The waves, which aren't breaking, bounce off Campbell Point, creating a cross-hatch wave effect. It is one of those days that it's easy to feel small on a big lake.

For forty-five minutes, we edge along the point, measuring each quartering wave, setting the canoe's angle, inching ahead. We are glad for our spray skirts. When we finally clear the tip of

Campbell Point, we turn and ride the following waves into the protection of Hattie Cove.

It's as if the big lake is reminding us who is in charge. It will get no argument from us.

KING OF THE COAST

D ay 10. Manitoba's Seal River. The six of us were sleeping
soundly in a plywood shack on Hudson Bay when some of
us were roused by an unfamiliar sound.

Duluth's Dan Theis seemed to regain consciousness first.

"Something's rooting around out there," Theis said.

Instantly, we were all sitting up in our sleeping bags, trying to
remember where we were and how we had gotten there. In the
weak light of dawn on this July morning, it didn't take us long
to guess what was happening.

A polar bear had stopped by to check out our canoes.

About 1,200 of these magnificent animals make their home
along the western shore of Hudson Bay. They prefer to be out
on the ice of the bay, where they can hunt seals, their principal
prey. But when the ice is gone during summer and early fall, the
bears must roam the coastline, foraging for whatever small
mammals they can find to sustain themselves.

Not that one would pass up a large mammal—say, a sinewy
canoeist—if one had a chance.

In our various stages of undress, we clambered out of our
bags and went to the door of the shack that had been built by
Jack Batstone of Churchill. Even in the low light, we could see
what was rooting around out there. It appeared to be a yearling
polar bear, not massive but plenty respectable.

"I saw him tip the green canoe over," said Theis, who had

been first to the door.

The canoes were about sixty feet from our cabin, pulled up well above the high-tide line. The bear was still inspecting the canoes—three Old Town Trippers.

Dave Baumgarten of Duluth grabbed his 12-gauge Remington 870 pump shotgun. It was one of two shotguns we had brought along. We could hear him loading buckshot and slugs into it. About that time, the bear left our canoes and began walking along the shore of the bay. When he got directly downwind of the shack, he turned and began walking toward us.

He appeared to be in no hurry, advancing at a deliberate pace. He walked in that fisher-like way that all polar bears walk—head slung low, front paws a bit pigeon-toed, with what seemed to be a swagger. Muscles rippled beneath his off-white coat. An impressive specimen.

The six of us were leaning out the door or peering out the window of the shack. When the bear was 35 feet from the cabin—we paced it off later that day—and still coming, Baumgarten had seen enough.

"I think this guy needs a warning shot fired near him, don't you?"

Concurrence was swift. Baumgarten fired a load of buckshot directly in front of the bear, kicking up a spray of sand. The bear did a quick spin and took off up the coast, headed north. We never saw him again.

We were thrilled to have encountered a bear and equally thrilled the encounter worked out as well as it did. We had babied those shotguns down the river for ten days, and Baumgarten's performed its intended purpose when the time arose.

Other canoeists we know have been visited by polar bears

along the shore of Hudson Bay, some at close range. But none of the paddlers we know has been injured.

However, I interviewed two canoeists who had paddled down a Hudson Bay tributary in 1983 and had camped on an island in the river near the bay to get a feel for the tides. A polar bear working the river's shoreline caught their scent and swam upriver to their island. The men had a shotgun, and they loaded it, taking refuge atop a large rock. The bear kept coming. The canoeists didn't want to shoot it.

When the bear finally reached point-blank range and was coming up the rock at them, the second canoeist shouted to his partner with the gun, "Shoot him!" The other canoeist pulled the trigger, dropping the bear dead mere feet away.

Life can be interesting when you're not at the top of the food chain.

JACKFISH, EH?

Trolling across Manitoba's Knee Lake, I could see my wife's fishing rod suddenly begin whipping toward the stern.

"I have one," Phyllis announced, setting the hook.

We were enjoying a layover day during a month-long trip that would take us down the Gods River to Hudson Bay. Phyllis and I had decided to snap on some spoons and see if we could find some of the northern pike—"jackfish" in Canada—for which Knee Lake was known.

"I'll reel up and get out of your way," I told Phyllis.

But wouldn't you know it? I had a hit myself while I was reeling up.

"You're on your own," I said. "I've got one, too."

Both pike kept fighting, and we kept reeling, gaining a little all the time. The closer we brought our fish to the boat, the more it appeared our lines were crossed. I hoped the sharp jaws of one of those northerns wouldn't cut one of our lines.

Not to worry. The same four-pound northern pike had taken each of our spoons. There was no second fish. Just one very hungry—or very aggressive—pike with the hooks of two spoons in its jaw.

Fishing isn't always that good on northern river trips. We've been on some trips where turbulent runoff made fishing entirely unproductive. And we've fished some good-looking water below rapids that should have held fish but didn't.

If you keep the rods handy, though, sooner or later you're likely to come across some of the best fishing you'll ever experience. There was a night on Ontario's Pipestone River when a black and gold Rapala took a two-pound walleye on every drift. Spinners and flies produced plenty of Arctic grayling at a camp on Manitoba's Seal River one afternoon. I've taken lake trout on dry flies while fishing a lake in Alaska's Brooks Range.

I like to fish, but Tom Bell and Dave Baumgarten are true anglers. On Manitoba's Bloodvein River, they could whip down a set of rapids, break out their rods and have caught their first walleye almost before the rest of us had finished scouting the rapids. Their lure of preference was a chartreuse twister-tail on a jig attached to a single-blade spinnerbait. We never haul live bait on our trips.

Bell and Baumgarten were along when we paddled the Poplar River in 1997. One afternoon, we pulled over to take a break on a smooth rock. The river funneled through a narrows there, and Bell knew it was the kind of place a walleye would live. He tossed a jig into the current and let it sink. When he felt the hit, he set the hook. In a couple of minutes, he had landed a chunky three-pound walleye. We were a few hours from making camp, so he released it.

I thought that looked like fun, so I tossed a quarter-ounce jig into the current. I had jigged it just a couple of times, when I felt a fish take it. The hit didn't feel especially vicious, but when the fish began running with the jig, it went upstream. A lot of current was pouring through those narrows. Must have been a nice walleye, I thought.

Then, the fish turned and went downstream. Fast. Much

faster than any walleye with which I've ever done battle. By now, my partners had gathered to watch. The fish took my line so far downstream I was sure he would never stop. It had to be a jackfish, eh? I had new eight-pound-test line on my reel, and I put all the pressure on the fish I dared. Finally, the line stopped leaving my reel.

He made a couple of runs like that. When you've spent most of your fishing life catching fish that weigh a pound or two, with the rare five- or six-pounder thrown in, it is hard to describe what it feels like to catch a truly large fish. The power of a big fish is amazing. It's like having your line hooked to a bicycle with Lance Armstrong pedaling away from you. In such a situation, you feel the battle is much more in the hands of the fish than the fisherman.

I worked the pike close a couple of times, and finally he came alongside the rock. Baumgarten tried to land him barehanded, but the big northern powered out of his grasp. We had no landing net.

Eventually, I brought the pike to the rock again, and this time Baumgarten landed him. We gawked in disbelief. Everything about the pike seemed oversized—his head, the breadth of his back, his frightening jaws. We measured him at 44 inches and let him go after a couple of photos. It took a minute to revive him, and I felt almost sick pondering the notion that we might have to keep that magnificent creature. But he finally gathered his strength and, with a swish of his massive tail, became part of the river again. Back home, a length-weight formula told us we had been looking at 24 pounds of pike.

Nice fish, as they say on the TV shows.

Every now and then, I happen onto the photos of myself holding that northern pike. Maybe my kids will be glad to have them someday. But the pictures always disappoint me.

That jack was much bigger than it looks, eh?

EXTORTION ON THE WINISK

The village of Webequie sits on an island in Winisk Lake, through which the Winisk River flows on its way to Hudson Bay. David Spencer and I pulled our Old Town Tripper up a small wooden ramp on the west side of the island one morning in the summer of 1991.

We had come ten days down the Pipestone River to its confluence with the Winisk on Winisk Lake, and we stopped at the community of 585 Ojibwa to see if we might purchase some beadwork moccasins or gauntlet mitts for those we'd left behind.

As it turned out, the day was windy and several thunderstorms moved through, so we ended up staying around town all day. We left our canoe and gear by the small ramp, unattended, trusting we had nothing anyone in the village might want.

It was a good day. We asked around town about who might have some moccasins or mitts to sell, and we were ushered to the homes of several women who did that kind of work. While we waited in front rooms watching satellite television programs, the woman of the home would go to a back room and bring out a cardboard box or plastic bag full of her work. The beadwork was beautiful, and there were moccasins of all sizes as well as some mitts. The moccasins and mitts were trimmed in rabbit fur. Spencer and I knew they would be a hit back home.

For a while, we also sat on a dock on the windward side of the island and watched young Ojibwa boys jump off the dock into the rolling waves. None of the boys wore a swimming suit. All of them had just peeled off their pants and were swimming in their briefs. If any one of them knew English, he chose not to speak it. The boys would mutter in Ojibwa and shout like boys anywhere having such a good time.

Spencer has a beard, and at one point, one of the boys ventured up to him and stroked his beard. Others quickly followed, rubbing their hands on his shaggy face. Finally, one of the boys spoke the only English words we heard them say: "Santa Claus." They all laughed.

We moseyed over to the band office to ask if anyone there knew of other women who had beadwork they wanted to sell. A teenage girl told us to wait in the office's conference room, a large meeting room with a couple of picnic tables in it. She burst out the door and went running up the village's main dirt road. We would learn later she had gone to the island radio station, a building hardly larger than an outhouse, where the lone disc jockey interrupted the day's music to announce our request.

Soon we saw a woman in a blue print dress and a scarf walking down the road toward the band office. She carried a plastic grocery bag. She was the first to arrive with her inventory of beadwork creations. Then came another woman and another. Soon, six or seven Ojibwa women were lined up along a wall of the meeting room, chatting amiably and laughing. We couldn't understand anything they said.

One by one, they had laid their wares on the tables until now it looked as if we were at the Webequie version of JC Penney. Spencer and I were a little overwhelmed. Having already purchased a few items on our earlier rounds, we hadn't intended to

buy much more. Now we found ourselves in an awkward situation. We hadn't expected that every woman in Webequie who
did beadwork would show up with all her goods.

There were many handsome and well-made items, beadwork
moccasins with floral and bird designs, magnificent gauntlet
mitts with the same colorful designs, even a couple of winter
caps lined with thick beaver fur.

I told the teenage girl to please convey our appreciation to all
the women and tell them we weren't prepared to buy much. She
translated that message to them. More chatting and laughing. I
told Spencer I thought they were laughing at how dirty his trail
pants were.

Spencer bought the beaverskin caps for his boys, and we each
bought some more moccasins. Our packs were going to be
bulging. We asked if we could have our pictures taken with the
women, and they consented somewhat self-consciously. Then
they trundled off down village roads with their bags.

It was now getting to be late afternoon, and we were ready to
head out and make camp. It always feels a little odd to find
yourself in a village with telephones and television and other
trappings of civilization in the middle of a wilderness trip. We
were ready to be back on the water, to find a camp on some
little beach and pitch our tent.

When we returned to the canoe, I couldn't find my fishing
tackle box. I knew I'd left it right under my seat in the bow. I
asked Spencer if he'd taken it as some kind of prank, but I
doubted it. No, he said. He didn't have it.

I looked again. No tackle. We'd been picked clean.

The Winisk River offers tremendous brook trout fishing, and

sampling it was one of the main purposes of our trip. I had packed along plenty of bucktail spinners and small spoons with that in mind. Now, they were gone. Spencer had brought no tackle, leaving that to me.

We considered our options. He stayed with the canoe while I hotfooted it down to the Hudson Bay Post—the Northern Store, as they're now called—to see what kind of tackle I could buy. The store had a few Dardevle spoons, most about the size of shovels. I bought a few smaller cheap spoons, but I would rather have had some spinners.

On my way past a baseball diamond on my way back to the canoe, I saw a game in progress. I stopped at one dugout—a wooden bench—and explained my plight. I offered twenty dollars to anyone who came up with my tackle box. But I got no takers. These kids were teenagers, boys and girls. They were having too much fun. They didn't want my money.

Dejectedly, I headed back to the canoe. There I found Spencer reclining in the stern seat, hands clasped behind his head. He pointed to the tackle box, sitting on top of a pack. Almost all of my tackle was there. A couple of Rapalas were missing, but we could do without those.

"Where'd that come from?" I asked him.

"A couple of young boys came by," Spencer said. "I offered them each five dollars if they could produce the tackle box. Extortion money."

Funny thing. These boys had reappeared with the tackle box in about five minutes, Spencer said. He paid them off. We were set to go.

The inside of the tackle box was littered with small leaves, pieces of grass and twigs. I could just see a group of little boys, digging through our tackle in some willow copse down by the water, arguing over who would take what, spilling the contents and refilling the box again.

I hope those two boys spent their extortion money well. And I hope the Rapalas caught fish for them.

MASON CAMP

Now this was different. We were in the middle of the Manitoba bush, and right in the heart of camp on the Seal River was a stone monument topped with a bronze plaque.

We had read about this spot. The plaque was a tribute to legendary wilderness paddler Bill Mason of Canada. We had all read his books and watched his paddling videos. Other wilderness paddlers had erected this modest tribute to Mason in memory of his contributions to canoeing.

Mason would have liked this camp. It lay high above the river on a shelf of fine gravel. The Seal, perhaps a quarter of a mile wide, slid past the camp forty feet below us. It had been a workout getting the packs and canoes up the steep bank.

This was esker country. The gravel shelf where we pitched our tents was an esker—the gravel deposits of a river that once flowed beneath a glacier. When the glaciers melted about twelve thousand years ago, they left behind these gravel ridges snaking across the land like raised veins on the back of a hand.

Above and behind our camp, another esker led away into the scruffy wilderness. After we made camp and gathered wood, we took off to hike it. It's rare on wilderness trips in the Canadian bush to be able to walk far at all from camp. These eskers, stretching for miles, gave us a feeling of freedom we had never experienced before.

Up on top, the esker was firm and easy to walk on. It was

almost like hiking a country road, except this road was littered with thousands of caribou droppings and lots of shed caribou antlers in every phase of decay. Atop the esker grew dwarf fireweed, every bit as brilliant pink as the full-size version we knew in Minnesota. But these were just four or five inches tall.

Dave Baumgarten and I sauntered along, inspecting antlers, scanning the distant ridges. In places, we could glimpse the river far away and far below us. The esker ran straight as a road for long stretches, then would bend a bit and take off on a new tangent. This was the "Land of Little Sticks," or stunted spruce trees. None grew tall enough to impede our view from this lofty highway.

Walking along, I tried to imagine a lobe of ice two miles thick lying atop this esker. I tried to imagine the cold, silty river flowing beneath it, depositing the gravel upon which we were now strolling. The afternoon was warm and muggy, and it was difficult visualizing this country in its ice-bound state.

Baumgarten and I picked up the occasional caribou antler and draped them over our shoulders as we walked. Our choices were almost infinite. We would think we had just the right one, only to discard it for one we deemed bigger or more perfectly formed.

The caribou themselves were presumably far north of here, on their calving grounds or moving slowly southward with their newborn calves. They must have moved through here in the fall or winter. We saw none during our visit, though we felt their presence.

Baumgarten and I weren't the only ones fascinated with the antlers. Along with our four fellow paddlers, we returned to camp with far more antlers than we could hope to load in our canoes and take down the river to Hudson Bay. We piled the extras around the base of the Mason monument. When we packed up to leave that camp, we each took one antler and lashed it on top of our packs, securing the load under the spray skirts of our canoes.

At Churchill, after our trip, an employee of Calm Air helped us pack the antlers into a cardboard box for the flight back to Thompson, Manitoba. Surprisingly, they each made the trip home in good shape.

The antler I brought back has become a piece of organic decor in a back yard flower garden. I see it almost daily, except during the winters when it's buried under snow. Even then, the antler is serving a purpose. Mice and voles gnaw on its points, taking on calcium the caribou stored there years ago.

Every time I walk past that antler, I'm pulled back to the Mason camp on the Seal for a few seconds. I can see the Seal sliding past camp. I can see the stone monument.

And I can see the barren esker snaking to the horizon in the Land of Little Sticks.

THE JOURNEY HOME

Saying Goodbye to a River

Always, it comes down to this. The waiting. We are camped on the dusty banks of the Mackenzie River in Canada's Northwest Territories. We have put the Mountain River behind us, and where the Mountain joins the Mackenzie, we made our last camp.

It is a hot and dusty July day. We have strung our kitchen fly merely for the shade. Like Bedouins in the desert, we lie low, trying not to generate heat. We are waiting for our bush flight back to civilization. Dave Spencer and Dick Adams are standing naked in the Mackenzie up to their belly buttons, reading books and swatting flies. The rest of us laze about, reading or napping.

For eleven days, we have ridden a cold, wild river down from the mountains. Up high, where the river was small, we looked for the channels that offered the most water. As the river grew, we sought more conservative routes and still found all the current we wanted. The Mountain is a big, pushy piece of water.

We had a black timber wolf stroll through camp one afternoon. We watched Dall sheep skitter along sheer rock walls. We hadn't seen another human.

Now the paddling was over, and we were on someone else's timetable. We were waiting for a Twin Otter that would carry us back to the village of Norman Wells.

This part never gets easier.

My mind took me back to other waiting places. A slender

crescent of sand along the Winisk River with Spencer. The historic fur-trading post at York Factory, where the Gods River idles into Hudson Bay. The Ojibwa village of Bloodvein, where the river of that name delivers its payload to Lake Winnipeg.

In each case, these places marked our initial reacquaintance with what we affectionately call the "real world." For days on all these rivers and others, we were totally free. Nobody told us whether to run a set of rapids or portage. We made our best judgments, took our best shots and dealt with the consequences. We camped when we wanted to, ate when we were hungry, fished when we had time.

I rarely feel more alive, more completely connected with the universe, than when I am on the trail in the wilderness. It's always good to be in wild country, but only after several days do you finally settle into the sweet rhythm of the trail. The names of the days fall away, and life shifts entirely to present tense. We are simply somewhere in a vast, quiet land—working our way down an artery of water that few people ever travel.

My fellow paddlers and I have shared so many miles together, so many campfires, that as we travel, the memories come along with us. In that sense, the rivers begin to flow together and the trips intertwine. Was that the Poplar or the Pigeon where we found the grave marker? Was that the first or second Bloodvein trip when Gary got sick? What trip was it where the smoke from the forest fires was so thick?

Given enough time, we can come up with the answers, but I'm not sure it matters. What matters is that we are out there, somewhere, living in the moment.

We wear little welts on our necks where the black flies dined.

The backs of our hands turn leathery and brown. Callouses build on our palms. We inch along the wiggly blue line on the map, marking rapids and campsites for future reference.

Why would we want any of this to end? A soft bed at home? A drink with ice in it? A fresh salad or a steak? No. None of the above. We want for nothing out here. We have the river. We have driftwood for the fire. We have the woodsmoke and the sky and the raspy squawk of the terns.

So, when we beach the canoes for the last time, it is with more than a little sadness. At least for now, for this summer, for this river, it is over. Here is what we do: We step out of the canoes, and we move among each other, shaking hands. We have always done this.

"Good trip," one of us says.

"Good trip," comes the reply.

It's a ritual of sorts. But it's more than that. It's a look-you-in-the-eye acknowledgment that you would paddle almost anyplace with this crew.

We are still hundreds or thousands of miles from home, but the paddling is over. The camps, the rapids, the wildlife will take their place along with the memories from all the other trips. From here on, it's a matter of catching ferries, planes or trains.

And waiting.

There's no glory in the waiting, ears cocked for the sound of a floatplane engine or the low drone of a ferry. With the essence of the trip behind us, we all want to get home as soon as possible. But nearly always, something holds up the departure. Maybe the wind is too strong. Or an overnight storm has backed up the bush planes, and they're still playing catch-up. Or the train has been delayed by a track problem.

So, we kick back, trying not to have expectations. If we've finished our own books, we trade around so everyone has fresh reading material. We walk along the river. We tell stories. We speculate about the reason behind the delay.

Most places, while we wait, civilization comes elbowing its way back into our lives. The Mackenzie was kind to us. In a couple of days of waiting, we saw only two kayakers and a motorboat.

The Bloodvein, in 2004, was more typical. We had hauled out at the ferry landing to wait. A couple of Ojibwa kids from the village of Bloodvein came clattering down the road on their bikes, spraying gravel as they skidded to a halt at the landing.

"Ferry's gonna be late," one said.

The kids rode off again. Eventually, a pickup rolled up in a cloud of dust and parked. The truck was old and battered, its bed full of cargo for the ferry. More people arrived in cars. A semi with a long flatbed trailer took its place in the line. We sat quietly off to the side, near our canoes and gear.

All of this activity comes as something of a shock when the loudest sound you've heard for a couple of weeks is the cry of greater yellowlegs along the river. If someone wants to visit, we chat, but more often than not, the locals choose not to engage us.

Finally, that day at Bloodvein, the ferry rumbled around an island and into view. It nosed up to the landing and, with a great creaking of cables, dropped its steel gangplank.

It was time to make the final portage.

A WING AND A PRAYER

The Twin Otter skimmed the bare peaks of the Mackenzie Mountains in Canada's Northwest Territories. Six of us were sardined into the fuselage of the plane, and all of the gear we would need for two weeks on the Mountain River was crammed alongside of us. That included three Old Town Discovery canoes.

The air was hazy with the smoke of distant forest fires. In addition to the haze, tattered shreds of low clouds were sliding across some of the 7,000-foot peaks we passed. The drone of the plane was loud enough to make conversation difficult, so we sat mostly with our own thoughts, looking down at the river we'd soon be paddling.

Suddenly, the plane banked hard to the left, then leveled out again. Dave Spencer, one of my paddling partners, turned in his seat with eyes the size of golf balls. He could see through an opening in the cockpit curtains the sky ahead.

"There was a big-ass mountain right in front of us!" Spencer shouted.

We missed the mountain and made the rest of the flight without incident. None of us really knew how close a call we'd witnessed, and nobody asked the pilots about it after we landed at Willow Handle Lake. When you make canoe trips into remote country, you almost inevitably put your life in the hands of bush pilots you've never met before. You hope they're seasoned, but you never know for sure.

In more than twenty years of making such flights, we've never had a serious problem. Some of our pickup flights have been a little late, but that was usually because of bad weather. But when you're sitting on a stretch of Hudson Bay or some other distant waterway, and your flight is a day beyond the agreed date, it's easy to wonder. One paddler we know had led a crew down the Seal River in northern Manitoba and had spent five days on Hudson Bay awaiting a pickup. Turns out the pilot who had flown them in had reportedly lost his license while they were paddling to the bay. Finally, another pilot realized the party was out there and made the pickup.

Most pilots and bush flight services are extremely diligent and work around the vagaries of backcountry weather to keep their clients happy. We're happy to put our trust in them. If they say it's too nasty to fly, we're content to stay on the ground. But every now and then the elements conspire to put you in a situation you'd rather avoid.

Spencer and I had been on the Pipestone and Winisk rivers in northern Ontario for two weeks in 1992 and were awaiting a pickup on the Winisk. Thunderstorms had been moving through the area, so we weren't surprised that our flight was twelve hours late. No big deal. We loaded up the DeHavilland Beaver with our gear, and the pilot strapped the Old Town Tripper to the struts.

The flight back to Pickle Lake, Ontario, should have taken about an hour and a half, but took about two and a half. The pilot was dodging squalls and fighting a stiff crosswind. It was the roughest bush flight we'd ever made. The crosswind would catch the canoe lashed above the floats, causing the Beaver to whip violently. Up front, I managed to remain on good terms with my stomach, but when I glanced into the back seat, I could see Spencer wasn't faring as well. His gaze was locked straight ahead, and his lips were cinched tight.

We were really glad when we finally taxied up to the dock at the floatplane base in Pickle Lake, and I sensed the pilot was, too. But you never know with bush pilots. They rarely let on. Maybe a flight like that was no big deal. I thought I'd check it out.

"On a scale of one to ten," I asked him, "how rough was that flight?"

"That was an eight," he said. "I don't like it any rougher than that."

After our 175-mile paddle down the Mountain River in the Northwest Territories in 2001, six of us awaited our return flight on the Mackenzie River. The weather was unseasonably warm. We were to be picked up about 9:00 P.M. one evening, and we were packed up and ready. But the flight never came. Eventually, we unpacked tents and sleeping bags and turned in for the night.

The next morning dawned clear and warm again. We ate breakfast, packed up and made another round of bets about when our flight would arrive. We'd be quietly reading, ears cocked for the low hum of an approaching plane. Finally, the blue and yellow Twin Otter came boring through the blue sky, swooped to a landing and taxied to our beach.

As we loaded the plane, someone said to pilots, "Thought maybe you forgot about us."

"Nope," one of the pilots responded, shoving another pack into the tail of the plane.

We shuttled more gear to the plane.

"Any problems?" someone else asked.

"Oh, we had to rebuild this left engine," the pilot said. "We didn't finish it until late last night."

He mentioned something about still having a little trouble with a starter on the engine. All the gear loaded, we clambered into the plane, sweaty and full of river grit. One pilot turned to the other and said, "Cross your fingers." And he cranked on the starter.

Both engines rumbled to life. In less than an hour we touched down in Norman Wells.

WILD TO THE END

A few moments earlier, we had been lunching on crackers and peanut butter and jelly in the shelter of willows along the Seal River. Now were back on the water, riding some of the largest waves we had ever encountered.

We weren't in a set of rapids. We were just attempting to cross the river so that we would have more protection once it rounded a bend. The river was a half-mile wide at this point. The wind, which was blowing the tops off the waves, was quartering us from the stern. Every veteran paddler knows that's a nasty wind, and this one was living up to its billing.

We were little more than a day from the shores of Hudson Bay, and trees of any size were behind us. Now the river was fringed only with head-high willows. All morning, we had battled into a quartering headwind, hugging the shoreline. But shelter was scant.

On the crossing, each wave lifted the stern of our Old Town Tripper and then, as we descended toward the trough, it wanted to shove the stern to the side. Dave Spencer of Duluth was in the stern. I was in the bow. Somewhere, our four partners were battling the same conditions in their two Trippers, but Spencer and I had no time to check their progress. It was all we could do keep our canoe from corkscrewing itself into every trough between the waves.

Predictably, conditions had worsened as we left the modest

protection of our lunch spot. The farther we ventured out in our crossing, the more wind we caught and the bigger the waves grew.

We had enough experience to know what to do, but the size of the waves and the gusts of the wind were putting us near our safety threshold. When a wave wanted to broach us, I'd reach out and draw to counter the force of the water. I knew Spencer was using the same technique on the opposite side of the canoe in the stern.

But finally, draw strokes weren't doing the job.

"Post!" Spencer yelled.

I drove my blade deep in the water as far away from the canoe as I could reach. I braced it there, using all my strength to hold the paddle vertically. We couldn't afford to broach in these waves.

Spencer posted on the other side of the canoe for several long seconds. We repeated the technique for half the crossing.

"I was praying to all the old paddlers I knew in heaven to help us out," Spencer would say later.

The crossing seemed interminable but probably took no more than ten minutes. One canoe at a time, we completed the passage and took a measure of refuge around the bend.

Thanks to the benevolence of the paddlers in heaven—or just good fortune—we were now working southeast with the wind mostly behind us. At some point down this leg of the river, we knew we would have to cross again before the next bend. When we did, it was a wild ride. The canoe rode to the top of each following wave. My end would drop over and begin the long slide downhill. But no longer were the waves quartering us, so we didn't have to work so hard to stay aligned.

Once around the next bend, we could see the river was white with rapids. It was a broad boulder field with plenty of room to pick our way through. With the increased speed of the water and the tailwind still pushing us, we had to ratchet up our lead time to avoid obstacles.

It was an amazing sight. Every frothy wave was being smacked by the wind, shattering its white curl into a sheet of spray. The wind whipped the spray low over the water. This was happening in countless places across the entire breadth of the river. Nothing was static. Everything was in horizontal motion, creating a scene that almost resembled an Impressionist painting.

"I've never moved this fast through rapids before," Spencer hollered from the stern.

But we were under control now. We read the water, made our moves and were escorted downstream by the wind and the current.

We made camp that night on a rock shelf at the river's edge and toasted our good fortunes. Against the possibility of polar bears, we pitched our tents in a cluster and strung an alarm cord around the perimeter of camp. No bears came.

The winds hadn't abated the next morning. We paddled against them for a time, then took a final turn toward the bay. We sneaked the edge of Deaf Rapids on the left and stopped for lunch on a flat rock. The sun was out. The day was cool for late July.

We had just opened the lunch pack when the wind lifted Dan Theis's life jacket and deposited it in the river. At first, we thought we could just grab it, but the wind and current conspired to carry it away rapidly.

Forget lunch. We stowed the food pack, and all three canoes set off to find the life jacket, now out of sight in the rock-studded river. Somehow, we found the life jacket. During the search, we realized the tide was going out and the river was dropping fast. The Seal had split into braided channels around myriad islands, and we weren't sure our channel would hold water once the tide went out.

We decided to ride the outgoing tide as far as we could. We dodged rocks. We scraped ledges. We kept choosing channels that we hoped would allow us passage.

That final descent to the Bay was worth the entire trip. The river's gradient was so steep you could see yourself sliding down to the ocean. The ocean-green of the Bay appeared before us. The wind, howling so loud that conversation among canoes was nearly impossible, kept shoving us toward the ocean.

Suddenly, the sky was full of eiders—large ducks that live along the coastline. They rose into the air in what seemed a massive spiral and circled over us as we made our descent.

The water was moving. The air was racing past us. The land was falling away. And now the sky was churning with a vortex of waterfowl.

The urgency of the departing tide drove us on and somehow, imperceptibly, the river became Hudson Bay. We found the humble plywood shack where we were to await our boat ride to Churchill. We drove the canoes onto the fine brown sand of the beach.

Tomorrow, we would paddle with belugas.

A SENSE OF URGENCY

For two days now, we had been paddling with beluga whales at the mouth of the Seal River on Hudson Bay. We had been on the river for eleven days, and now we were waiting for Jack.

Almost everyone who paddles the Seal River waits for Jack Batstone on the tidal flats at the river's mouth. Jack is the entrepreneur from Churchill, forty miles south, who offers a boat shuttle for paddlers who don't want to paddle that much ocean in their canoes.

Jack had been kind enough to let the six of us use his plywood shack at the river's mouth while we awaited his pickup. It wasn't much, but it was the only structure in sight on the coastal lowland where polar bears made regular visits. We had asked Jack, before the trip, whether the shack was bear-proof.

"Five-eighths-inch plywood," Jack had said. "Takes 'em a while to get through that."

Jack was now one day overdue for our pickup, but we weren't concerned. The wind had blown about fifty miles per hour all day the previous day. We knew Jack wouldn't attempt the trip in those conditions. Today wasn't bad. Dan Theis and Dick Adams had decided to paddle about four miles up the coast to an ecotourism base we had heard about.

They were on their way back when they saw a large open skiff on the Bay. A man stood in the bow. At intervals, he shouldered a shotgun and fired at the sky. Theis and Adams paddled over to check things out. That's how they met Jack.

The rest of us had seen the boat from our perch atop the roof of Jack's shack. We assumed it was Jack. We were already scurrying around, throwing loose gear in our Duluth packs when Theis and Adams paddled up.

"What's with the shooting?" someone asked.

"Jack is feeling a sense of urgency," Theis said. "He doesn't like the weather. He was using a lot of expletives."

We had to chuckle. The Seal had already thrown all kinds of nasty weather at us, and a polar bear had come calling two nights before. Jack's urgency represented just one more hurdle for us.

The cause of Jack's urgency was his fear that the wind was going to switch to the northeast, which would make for an ugly ride back to Churchill. We loaded our canoes and made the choppy paddle a half-mile out to Jack's boat. He didn't want to venture closer to shore because the Bay is so shallow and rocky. As we got close to the boat, it was obvious Jack was in a tizzy.

"I don't like this," he kept saying, looking over his shoulder at the waves. "I don't like this."

We threw our gear into his 23-foot open boat, then clambered in and hauled two of the canoes aboard.

"I don't like this," Jack said. "I don't like taking six people and three canoes with this boat."

We wondered, silently, why Jack had signed up for the job if he didn't feel comfortable with his boat's capacity. But this wasn't the time to discuss that matter. We tied the third canoe on a towrope and cast it astern. Jack fired up his big Yamaha, and we were off, the third canoe dancing in our wake.

It always feels odd to reach this part of a wilderness trip, the part in which we no longer play a role in controlling our destiny. After being totally self-propelled and self-sufficient for a couple of weeks, we are suddenly like cattle in a truck. It doesn't matter whether we're flying out in some bush plane or crossing Hudson Bay in Jack's skiff. We must put our faith in the hands of some pilot or some boat captain we don't know and trust him to get us where we're going.

Jack's fears did not materialize. The wind did not shift, and we were riding big but smooth swells. Jack seemed to be more comfortable. Slowly, the grain elevators of Churchill nosed above the horizon, and we could see our destination.

The swells were rolling under us from port to starboard. It's hard to say how big they were. Six or eight feet, probably. For several seconds, we would ride the top of a swell, then slide down its flank into a broad trough. Jack's boat handled the swells easily.

A couple of us, close enough to be heard over the motor, spoke to Jack occasionally. But we were spread out throughout the boat, and mostly we were alone with our thoughts. The best part of the journey was behind us. Already, we had begun to think of the trip in past tense. Rolling over the swells of Hudson Bay, we silently reflected on the river we had left behind, the spirited grayling we had caught, the eskers we had walked, the rapids we had run. I couldn't speak for the others, but I felt a sadness upon leaving all of that behind. There is a part of me that never wants these trips to end.

The other part of me wanted to be home with my wife and children as soon as possible. I wanted to get off Jack's boat in Churchill and be whisked home in seconds. I was ready for some hugs. As I listened to the drone of Jack's Yamaha outboard, I envisioned the faces of my wife and son and daughter. But they would have to wait for a couple of days.

I looked at my buddies, heads bobbing and swaying with the movement of the boat. We had been paddlers. Now we were merely passengers. Jack's cargo.

Over the bow, the grain elevators of Churchill were looking taller all the time.

BRINGING IT BACK

My friend and fellow writer Jeff Rennicke has an expression. "Some of my friends have photographic memories," he says. "Mine is spiral-bound."

Rennicke has backpacked and rafted extensively in Alaska and the American West. The stories and books he has written about those trips are full of rich details. The details come out of little notebooks he carries in his pocket on those trips.

But you don't have to be a writer to appreciate the value of keeping notes or journals on your travels. Even a few hastily scribbled notes made each day can help you recall a particular set of rapids, a challenging moment or a memorable camp years later.

My journals, like Rennicke's, are typically spiral-bound notebooks small enough to fit in a zip-top bag. I keep one tucked in my daypack. On some trips, I also carry a smaller, pocket-sized notebook in my shirt pocket, although that comes with a risk. If we happen to take an unscheduled swim in a set of rapids, I know I'll be spending time drying the notebook out come evening.

The value of a trip journal appreciates over time. Memories fade, soften around the edges. But a journal entry brings the details of a day back into clarity, like this one from my first trip, on the Gods River almost 24 years ago:

Day 9, Sunday, July 24, 1983—Hell of a day... Drug the canoes

*over two beaver dams and found what we were looking for—
our two-mile portage from Bayly (Lake) to Gods (Lake). Started
the portage at 9:30 A.M. and finished at 2:15 P.M. Hardest
portage, by far, that I've ever made in my life. Half or more of
it was ankle- to knee-deep bog... I cannot describe how hard it
was to carry the canoe or a single pack through the bog. Every
step was like stepping into a pile of oats: The bog simply folded
in over boot-tops, then boots. Then came the suction as you
tried to pull the boot out. I went in to my knee twice and had to
stop and pull my leg out. Phyl went in twice to mid-thigh and
had to put the pack down so she could get back up. It is as tired
as I've ever been outside of running a marathon.*

It isn't always easy to make myself write in my journal daily.
I can remember crawling in the tent totally exhausted at the end
many long days. All I wanted to do was collapse in my sleeping
bag. I had to force myself to scratch out a few notes. But I've
rarely missed a day because I know I'll appreciate having the
entry later.

Different people I've traveled with over the years chose different times of day to write. Will Steger, the polar adventurer
from Ely, Minnesota, writes first thing in the morning when he's
drinking tea in the tent. Some paddlers write at midday, while
taking a short rest after lunch. On many of the trips our crew
has made, we'll write before dinner, sitting along the river while
sipping Scotch or brandy. It all works.

Here's a partial entry from the Mountain River in 1999:

*Thursday, July 8, 1999—We saw a full-grown timber wolf on
the left shore on a small gravel bar at mid-morning in the gray
and overcast. Very cool. I saw him walking on the bar, nose to
the ground. Gray and some darker fur. When he saw us, no
more than fifty feet away, he came to the edge of the bar and put
his front paws up on a small stump of a downed tree. He perked
his ears up and stared at us as we coasted by.*

More than words go into my journals. I'm a pitiful artist, but sometimes I'll make a sketch to describe a set of rapids. I often jot down precise quotes from my fellow travelers at poignant moments because I know I won't remember them accurately later. Some of my journals are stuffed with physical mementoes from the trail—a single mountain avens, a tuft of Arctic cotton grass, a sprig of dwarf birch. Though ironed flat by the pages and desiccated by time, they always yank me right back to the country from which they came.

In a more pragmatic effort, I'll usually list at the back of the journal some notes for future trips—a new piece of trail clothing I'd like to have, a particularly good meal idea, some packing technique I've learned from one of my fellow paddlers.

Sometimes, too, I'll record a passage from a book I was reading at the time, or a selection someone else read aloud in camp. Here's one from the Tana River (Alaska) in 1995:

> *In this wilderness life, I have found a way to touch the world once more. One way. To live the life that is here to be lived, as nearly as I can without that other—clock hands, hours and wages. I relive each day the ancient expectation of the hunt—the setting out and the trail at dawn. What will we find today?*
>
> —*John Haines, 'The Stars, The Snow, The Fire'*

You would have trouble reading my journals. My hand-writing is poor. Sometimes even I puzzle for a few seconds over a word written too hastily or under the weight of weariness fifteen or twenty years ago. But eventually I figure it out. At home, my journals are filed away on a shelf, spiral-bound memories of places far away. Sometimes, on a winter night, I'll pull one down on a whim, pick a page, and begin reading.

Suddenly, I am there. On the Bloodvein or the Steel or the

Lake Superior shore of Ontario's Pukaskwa National Park. I can almost smell the woodsmoke. I can hear the whisper of the river passing by. I can see my companions on a rock ledge, scouting a set of rapids. I can feel the cold rain at a midday pullover.

My journals remind me that I am a rich man.

WILDERNESS TRIPS

Here is a chronological list of the northern trips that a group of us have made over the past years and that provided much of the material for the essays in this book.

1983   Three-week canoe trip to Hudson Bay
on Manitoba's **Gods River**.

1990   Four-day sea-kayaking trip on **Lake Superior**
in Ontario's Pukaskwa National Park.

1991   Two-week trip on the **Pipestone** and
Winisk rivers in northern Ontario.

1992   Week-long canoe trip on **Lake Superior**
in Ontario's Pukaskwa National Park.

1993   Eight-day trip on Manitoba's **Bloodvein River**,
a tributary of Lake Winnipeg.

1994   Six-day trip on Ontario's **Steel River**,
a tributary of Lake Superior.

1995   Two-week raft trip on the **Tana** and **Chitina** rivers
in Wrangell-St. Elias National Park, Alaska.

1997   Week-long canoe trip on Manitoba's
Poplar River, a tributary of Lake Winnipeg.

1998   Two-week trip on the **Seal River** to
Hudson Bay in northeastern Manitoba.

1999   Two-week trip on the **Mountain River**
in Canada's Northwest Territories.

2000   Eight-day trip on Manitoba's **Pigeon River**,
a tributary of Lake Winnipeg.

2003   Twelve-day trip on the **Nigu River**
in Gates of the Arctic National Park, Alaska.

2004   Eight-day trip on Manitoba's **Bloodvein River**,
a tributary of Lake Winnipeg.

2006   Week-long trip on the **White River**, a
Lake Superior tributary in Ontario.

105 100 95

Seal R.

Churchill

Reindeer Lake

Lynn Lake

MANITOBA

55

Thompson

Gods Lake G R

Oxford House

SASKATCHEWAN

Lake Winnipeg

Poplar R.

Pigeon R.

Bloodvein R.

50

Winnipeg

CANADA
U.S.

105

NORTH DAKOTA

MINNESOT

100 95